The
Kamasutra
of Vatsyayana

The
Kamasutra
of Vatsyayana

Lustre Press
·
Roli Books

ISBN: 81-7437-063-3

Photographs of paintings from the private collection of Kanwar Sangram Singh of Nawalgarh
Photographs on pages 19, 35, 39, 43, 47, 51, 62, 67, 75, 87 from the Juna Mahal Palace in Dungarpur
Cover and photographs on pages 15, 27, 31, 70, 71 © Lustre Press
Photographers: Aditya Patankar, Subhash Bhargava, M.D. Sharma

© **Lustre Press Pvt. Ltd. 1992**
Third impression 2000
M-75, Greater Kailash-II Market, New Delhi-110 048, INDIA
Phones: (011) 6442271, 6462782, 6460886, Fax: (011) 6467185
E-mail: roli@vsnl.com, Website: rolibooks.com

Typeset in Palatino by Excel Computers Services, New Delhi

Printed and bound in Singapore by Star Standard Industries (Pte.) Ltd.

Title page: Men should study the *Kama Sutra* and the arts subordinate thereto . . . a man who is versed in these arts, who is loquacious and acquainted with the arts of gallantry, gains very soon the hearts of women, even though he is only acquainted with them for a short time.

CONTENTS

Introduction

IT may be interesting to some persons to learn how it came about that Vatsyayana was first brought to light and translated into the English language. It happened thus. While translating with the pundits the *Anunga Runga*, or the Stages Of Love, reference was frequently found to be made to one Vatsya. The sage Vatsya was of this opinion, or that opinion. The sage Vatsya said this, and so on. Naturally questions were asked who the sage was, and the pundits replied that Vatsya was the author of the standard work on love in Sanscrit literature, that no Sanscrit library was complete without his work, and that it was most difficult now to obtain in its entire state. The copy of the manuscript obtained in Bombay was defective, and so the pundits wrote to Benares, Calcutta and Jeypoor for copies of the manuscript from Sanscrit libraries in those places. Copies having been obtained, they were then compared with each other, and with the aid of a commentary called *Jayamangla* a revised copy of the entire manuscript was prepared, and from this copy the English translation was made. The following is the certificate of the chief pundit:

'The accompanying manuscript is corrected by me after comparing four different copies of the work. I had the assistance of a commentary called *Jayamangla* for correcting the portion in the first five parts, but found great difficulty in correcting the remaining portion because, with the exception of one copy thereof which was tolerably correct, all the other copies I had were far too incorrect. However, I took that portion as correct in which the majority of the copies agreed with each other'.

The *Aphorisms On Love* by Vatsyayana contain about one thousand two hundred and fifty slokas or verses, and are divided into parts, parts into chapters, and sixty-four paragraphs. Hardly anything is known about the author. His real name is supposed to be Mallinaga or Mrillana, Vatsyayana being his family name. At the close of the work this is what he writes about himself:

'After reading and considering the works of Babhravya and other ancient authors, and thinking over the meaning of the rules given by them, this treatise was composed, according to the precepts of the Holy Writ, for the benefit of the world, by Vatsyayana, while leading the life of a religious student at Benares, and wholly engaged in the contemplation of the Deity. This book is not to be used merely as an instrument for satisfying our desires. A person acquainted with the true principles of this science, who preserves his *Dharma* (virtue or religious merit), his *Artha* (worldly wealth) and his *Kama* (pleasure or sensual gratification), and who has regard to the customs of the people, is sure to obtain the mastery over his senses. In short, an intelligent and

Facing page: The following are the kind of friends: one who has played with you in childhood; one who is of the same disposition and fond of the same things; one who is acquainted with your secrets and faults, and whose faults and secrets are also known to you. . .

knowing person, attending to *Dharma* and *Artha* and also to *Kama*, without becoming the slave of his passions, will obtain success in everything that he may do.

It is impossible to fix the exact date either of the life of Vatsyayana or of his work. It is supposed that he must have lived between the first and sixth century of the Christian era, on the following grounds: He mentions that Satkarni Satvahan, a king of Kuntal, killed Malayavati his wife with an instrument called *kartari* by striking her in the passion of love, and Vatsya quotes this case to warn people of the danger arising from some old customs of striking women when under the influence of this passion. Now this king of Kuntal is believed to have lived and reigned during the first century AD, and consequently Vatsya must have lived after him. On the other hand, Virahamihira, in the eighteenth chapter of his *Brihatsamhita*, treats of the science of love, and appears to have borrowed largely from Vatsyayana on the subject. Now Virahamihira is said to have lived during the sixth century AD, and as Vatsya must have written his works previously, therefore not earlier than the first century AD, and not later than the sixth century AD, must be considered as the approximate date of his existence.

On the text of the *Aphorisms Of Love* by Vatsyayana, only two commentaries have been found, one called *Jayamangla* or *Sutrabashya*, and the other *Sutravritti*. The date of the *Jayamangla* is fixed between the tenth and thirteenth century AD, because while treating of the sixty-four arts an example is taken from the *Kavyaprakasha*, which was written about the tenth century AD. Again, the copy of the commentary procured was evidently a transcript of a manuscript which once had a place in the library of a Chalukyan king named Vishaladeva, a fact elicited from the following sentence at the end of it:

'Here ends the part relating to the art of love in the commentary on the *Vatsyayana Kama Sutra*, a copy from the library of the king of kings, Vishaladeva, who was a powerful hero, as it were a second Arjuna, and the head jewel of the Chalukya family'.

Now it is well known that this king ruled in Guzerat from 1244 to 1262 AD, and founded a city called Visalnagur. The date, therefore, of the commentary is taken to be not earlier than the tenth and not later than the thirteenth century. The author of it is supposed to be one Yashodhara, the name given him by his preceptor being Indrapada. He seems to have written it during the time of affliction caused by his separation from a clever and shrewd woman, at least that is what he himself says at the end of each chapter. It is presumed that he called his work after the name of his absent mistress, or the word may have some connection with the meaning of her name.

This commentary was most useful in explaining the true meaning of Vatsyayana, for the commentator appears to have had a considerable knowledge of the times of the older author, and gives in some places very minute information. This cannot be said of the other commentary, called *Sutravritti*, which was written about 1789 AD by Narsing Shastri, a pupil of a Sarveshwar Shastri; the latter was descendant of Bhaskar, and so also was our author, for at the conclusion of every part he calls himself Bhaskar Narsing Shastri. He was induced to write the work by order of the learned Raja Vrijalala, while he was residing in Benares, but as to the merits of this commentary it does not deserve much commendation. In many cases the writer does not appear to have understood the meaning of the original author, and has changed the text in many places to fit in with his own explanations.

An abridged translation of the original work now follows. It has been prepared in complete accordance with the text of the manuscript, and is given, without further comments, as made from it.

I

On Sexual Congress

I

Of the study of the Kama Shastra

Men should study the *Kama Sutra* and the arts and sciences subordinate thereto, in addition to the study of the arts and sciences contained in *Dharma* and *Artha*. Even young maids should study this *Kama Sutra* along with arts and sciences before marriage, and after it they could continue to do so with the consent of their husbands.

Here some learned men object, and say that females, not being allowed to study any science, should not study the *Kama Sutra*. But Vatsyayana is of the view that this objection does not hold good, for women already know the practice of *Kama Sutra*, and that practice is derived from the *Kama Shastra*, or the science of Kama itself. Moreover, it is not only in this but in many other cases that though the practice of a science is known to all, only a few persons are acquainted with the rules and laws on which the science is based. Thus the Yadnikas or sacrificers, though ignorant of grammar, make use of appropriate words when addressing the different deities, and do not know how these words are framed. Again, persons do the duties required of them on auspicious days, which are fixed by astrology, though they are not acquainted with the

science of astrology. In a like manner riders of horses and elephants train these animals without knowing the science of training animals, but from practice only. And similarly the people of the most distant provinces obey the laws of the kingdom from practice, and because there is a king over them, and without further reason. And from experience we find that some women, such as daughters of princes and their ministers, and public women, were actually versed in the *Kama Shastra*.

A female, therefore, should learn the *Kama Shastra*, or at least part of it, by studying its practice from some confidential friend. She should study alone in private the sixty-four practices that form a part of the *Kama Shastra*. Her teacher should be one of the following persons, viz. the daughter of a nurse brought up with her and already married, or a female friend who can be trusted in everything, or the sister of her mother (i.e. her aunt), or an old female servant, or a female beggar who may have formerly lived in the family, or her own sister, who can always be trusted.

The following are the arts to be studied, together with the *Kama Sutra*: singing; playing on

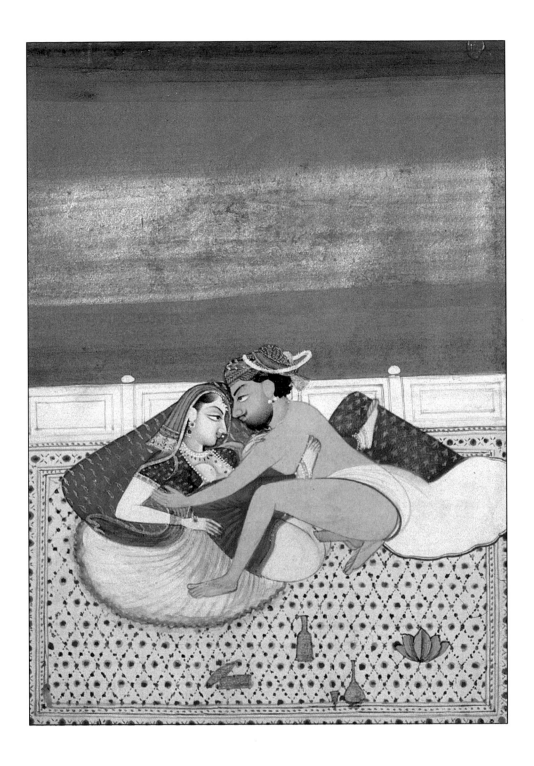

Above: . . . as girls are not acquainted with sexual union, they should be treated with the greatest delicacy, and the man should proceed with considerable caution. Women being of a tender nature, want tender beginnings. . .

Facing page: Young women should study the *Kama Sutra* along with its arts and sciences before marriage, and after it they could continue to do so with the consent of their husbands. Public women endowed with a good disposition, beauty and other winning qualities, and also versed in the above arts. . . can make their husbands favourable to them, even though these may have thousands of wives besides themselves.

musical instruments; dancing; union of dancing, singing, and playing instrumental music; writing and drawing; tattooing; arraying and adorning an idol with rice and flowers; spreading and arranging beds or couches of flowers, or flowers upon the ground; colouring the teeth, garments, hair, nails and body, i.e. staining, dyeing, colouring and painting the same; fixing stained glass into a floor; the art of making beds, and spreading out carpets and cushions for reclining; playing on musical glasses filled with water; storing and accumulating water in aqueducts, cisterns and reservoirs; picture making, trimming and decorating; stringing of rosaries, necklaces, garlands and wreaths; binding of turbans and chaplets, and making crests and top-knots of flowers; scenic representations; stage playing; art of making ear ornaments; art of preparing perfumes and odours; proper disposition of jewels and decorations, and adornment in dress; magic or sorcery; quickness of hand or manual skill; culinary art, i.e. cooking and cookery; making lemonades, sherbets, acidulated drinks, and spirituous extracts with proper flavour and colour; tailor's work and sewing; making parrots, flowers, tufts, tassels, bosses, knobs etc. out of yarn or thread; solution of riddles, enigmas, covert speeches, verbal puzzles and enigmatical questions; the art of mimicry or imitation; reading, including chanting and intoning; study of sentences difficult to pronounce; practice with sword, single stick, quarter staff and bow and arrow; drawing inferences, reasoning and inferring; carpentry; architecture, or the art of building; knowledge about gold and silver coins, and jewels and gems; chemistry and mineralogy; colouring jewels, gems and beads; knowledge of mines and quarries; gardening: knowledge of treating the diseases of trees and plants, of nourishing them, and determining their ages; art of cock fighting, quail fighting and ram fighting; art of teaching parrots and starlings to speak; art of applying perfumed ointments to the body, and of dressing the hair with unguents and perfumes and braiding it; art of understanding writing in cypher, and the writing of words in a peculiar way; art of speaking by changing the forms of words, by changing the beginning and end of words, adding unnecessary letters between every syllable of a word, and so on; knowledge of language and of the vernacular dialects; art of making flower carriages; art of framing mystical diagrams, of addressing spells and charms, and binding armlets; mental exercises, such as completing stanzas or verses on receiving a part of them; composing poems; knowledge of dictionaries and vocabularies; knowledge of ways of changing and disguising the appearance of persons; knowledge of ways of changing the appearance of things, such as making cotton to appear as silk, coarse and common things to appear as fine and good; various ways of gambling; art of obtaining possession of the property of others by means of mantras or incantations; skill in youthful sports; knowledge of the rules of society, and of how to pay respect and compliments to others; knowledge of the art of war, of arms, of armies, etc; knowledge of scanning or constructing verses; arithmetical recreations; making artificial flowers; making figures and images in clay.

A public woman endowed with a good disposition, beauty and other winning qualities, and also versed in the above arts, obtains the name of a Ganika, or public woman of high quality, and receives a seat of honour in an assemblage of men. She is, moreover, always respected by the king, and praised by learned men, and her favour being sought for by all, she becomes an object of universal regard. The daughter of a king too, as well as the daughter of a minister, being learned in the above arts, can make their husbands favourable to them, even though these may have thousands of other wives besides themselves. And in the same manner, if a wife becomes separated from her husband, and falls into distress, she can support herself easily, even in a foreign country, by means of her knowledge of these arts. Even the bare knowledge of them gives attractiveness to a woman, though the practice of them may be only possible or otherwise according to the circumstances of each case. A man who is versed in these arts, who is loquacious and acquainted with the arts of gallantry, gains very soon the hearts of women, even though he is only acquainted with them for a short time.

II

Of the life of a citizen

Having thus acquired learning, a man, with the wealth that he may have gained by gift, conquest, purchase, deposit, or inheritance from his ancestors, should become a householder, and pass the life of a citizen. He should take a house in a city, or large village, or in the vicinity of good men, or in a place which is the resort of many persons. This abode should be situated near some water, and divided into different compartments for different purposes. It should be surrounded by a garden, and also contain two rooms, an outer and an inner one. The inner room should be occupied by the females, while the outer room, balmy with rich perfumes, should contain a bed, soft, agreeable to the sight, covered with a clean white cloth, low in the middle part, having garlands and bunches of flowers upon it, and a canopy above it, and two pillows, one at the top, another at the bottom. There should be also a sort of couch besides, and at the head of it a sort of stool, on which should be placed the fragrant ointments for the night, as well as flowers, pots containing collyrium and other fragrant substances, things used for perfuming the mouth, and the bark of the common citron tree. Near the couch, on the ground, there should be a pot for spitting, a box containing ornaments, and also a lute hanging from a peg made from the tooth of an elephant, a board for drawing, a pot containing perfume, some books, and some garlands of yellow amaranth flowers. Not far from the couch and on the ground, there should be a round seat, a toy cart, and a board for playing with dice; outside the outer room there should be cages of birds, and a separate place for spinning, carving and such like diversions. In the garden there should be a whirling swing and a common swing, as also a bower of creepers covered with flowers, in which a raised parterre should be made for sitting.

Now the householder, having got up in the morning and performed his necessary duties, should wash his teeth, apply a limited quantity of ointments and perfumes to his body, put some ornaments on his person and collyrium on his eyelids and below his eyes, colour his lips with alacktaka, and look at himself in the glass. Having then eaten betel leaves, with other things that give fragrance to the mouth, he should perform his usual business. He should bathe daily, anoint his body with oil every other day, apply a lathering substance to his body every three days, get his head (including face) shaved every four days, and the other parts of his body every five or ten days. All these things should be done without fail, and the sweat of the armpits should also be removed. Meals should be taken in the forenoon, in the afternoon, and again at night, according to Charayana. After breakfast, parrots and other birds should be taught to speak, and the fighting of cocks, quails and rams should follow. A limited time should be devoted to diversions with Pithamardas, Vitas and Vidushakas, and then should be taken the midday sleep. After this the householder, having put on his clothes and ornaments should, during the afternoon, converse with his friends. In the evening there should be singing, and after that the householder, along with his friend, should await in his room, previously decorated and perfumed, the arrival of the woman that may be attached to him, or he may send a female messenger for her, or go for her himself. After her arrival at his house, he and his friend should welcome her, and entertain her with loving and agreeable conversation. Thus end the duties of the day.

The following are the things to be done occasionally as diversions or amusements: holding festivals in honour of different deities; social gatherings of both sexes; drinking parties, picnics, other social diversions.

Above: When the wife wants to approach her husband in private, her dress should consist of many ornaments, various kinds of flowers, and a cloth decorated with different colours, and some sweet-smelling ointments or unguents.

Facing page: A girl who is much sought after should marry the man she likes, and whom she thinks would be obedient to her, and capable of giving her pleasure.

III

Of different kinds of congress and love quarrels

In the pleasure room, decorated with flowers, and fragrant with perfumes, attended by his friends and servants, the citizen should receive the woman, who will come bathed and dressed, and invite her to take refreshments and to drink freely. He should then seat her on his left side, and holding her hair, and touching also the end knot of her garment, he should gently embrace her with his right arm. They should then carry on an amusing conversation on various subjects, and may also talk suggestively of things which would be considered as coarse, or not to be mentioned generally in society. They may then sing, either with or without gesticulations, and play on musical instruments, talk about the arts, and persuade each other to drink. At last when the woman is overcome with love and desire, the citizen should dismiss the people that may be with him, giving them flowers, ointments, and betel leaves, and then when the two are left alone, they should proceed as has been described in the following chapters.

Such is the beginning of sexual union. At the end of the congress, the lovers with modesty, and not looking at each other, should go separately to the washing-room. After this, sitting in their own places, they should eat some betel leaves, and the citizen should apply with his own hand to the body of the woman some pure sandalwood ointment, or ointment of some other kind. He should then embrace her with his left arm, and with agreeable words should cause her to drink from a cup held in his own hand, or he may give her water to drink. They can then eat sweetmeats, or anything else, according to their liking, and may drink fresh juice, soup, gruel, extracts of meat, sherbet, the juice of mango fruits, the extract of the juice of the citron tree mixed with sugar, or anything that may be liked in different countries, and known to be sweet, soft, and pure. The lovers may also sit on the terrace of the palace or house, and enjoy the moonlight, and carry on an agreeable conversation. At this time, too, while the woman lies in his lap, with her face towards the moon, the citizen should show her the different planets, the morning star, the polar star, and the seven Rishis, or Great Bear. This is the end of sexual union.

Congress is of the following kinds: viz. loving congress; congress of subsequent love; congress of artificial love; congress of transferred love; congress like that of eunuchs; deceitful congress; congress of spontaneous love.

1) When a man and a woman, who have been in love with each other for some time, come together with great difficulty, or when one of the two returns from a journey, or is reconciled after having been separated on account of a quarrel, this congress is called the 'loving congress'. It is carried on according to the liking of the lovers, and as long as they choose.

2) When two persons come together, while their love for each other is still in its infancy, their congress is called the 'congress of subsequent love'.

3) When a man carries on the congress by exciting himself by means of the sixty-four ways, such as kissing, etc. or when a man and a woman come together, their congress is then called 'congress of artificial love'. At this time all the ways and means mentioned in the *Kama Shastra* should be used.

4) When a man, from the beginning to the end of the congress, though having connection with the woman, thinks all the time that he is enjoying another one whom he loves, it is called the 'congress of transferred love'.

5) Congress between a man and a female water carrier, or female servant of a caste lower than his own, lasting only until the desire is satisfied, is called 'congress like that of eunuchs'. Here external touches, kisses, and manipulations are not to be employed.

6) The congress between a courtesan and a rustic, and that between citizens and the women of villages, and bordering countries, is called 'deceitful congress'.

7) The congress that takes place between two persons who are attached to one another, and which is done according to their own liking, is called 'spontaneous congress'.

Thus ends the kinds of congress. We shall now speak of love quarrels.

A woman who is very much in love with a man cannot bear to hear the name of her rival mentioned, or to have any conversation regarding her, or to be addressed by her name through mistake. If such take place, a great quarrel arises, and the woman cries, becomes angry, tosses her hair about, strikes her lover, falls from her bed or seat and, casting aside her garlands and ornaments, throws herself down on the ground.

At this time, the lover should attempt to reconcile her with conciliatory words, and should take her up carefully and place her on her bed. But she, not replying to his questions, and with increased anger, should bend his head down by pulling his hair, and having kicked him once, twice, or thrice on his arms, head, bosom or back, should then proceed to the door of the room. Dattaka says that she should then sit angrily near the door and shed tears, but should not go out, because she would be found fault with for going away. After a time, when she thinks that the conciliatory words and actions of her lover have reached their utmost, she should then embrace him, talking to him with harsh and reproachful words, but at the same time showing a loving desire for congress.

When the woman is in her own house, and has quarrelled with her lover, she should go to him and show how angry she is, and leave him. Afterwards the citizen having sent the Vita, the Vidushaka or the Pithamudra to pacify her, she should accompany them back to the house, and spend the night with her lover. Thus ends the love quarrel.

A man, employing the sixty-four means mentioned by Babhravya, obtains his object, and enjoys women of the first quality. A man devoid of other knowledge, but well acquainted with the sixty-four divisions, becomes a leader in any society of men and women. He is looked upon with love by his own wife, by the wives of others, and by courtesans.

IV

Of kinds of sexual union

Man is divided into three classes viz. the hare man, the bull man, and the horse man, according to the size of his lingam. Woman also, according to the depth of her yoni, is either a female deer, a mare, or a female elephant. There are thus three equal unions between persons of corresponding dimensions, and there are six unequal unions, when the dimensions do not correspond, or nine in all.

In these unequal unions, when the male exceeds the female in point of size, his union with a woman who is immediately next to him in size is called high union, and is of two kinds; while his union with the woman most remote from him in size is called the highest union, and is of one kind only. On the other hand, when the female exceeds the male in point size, her union with a man immediately next to her in size is called the low union, and is of two kinds; while her union with a man most remote from her in size is called the lowest union, and is of one kind only.

In other words, the horse and mare, the bull and deer, form the high union, while the horse and deer forms the highest union. On the female side, the elephant and bull, the mare and hare, form low unions, while the elephant and the hare make lowest union.

There are, then, nine kinds of union according to dimensions. Amongst all these, equal unions are the best; those of a superlative degree, i.e. the highest and the lowest, are the worst, and the rest are middling, and with them the high are better than the low.

There are also nine kinds of union according to the force of passion or carnal desire, as follows: a man is called a man of small passion whose desire at the time of sexual union is not great, whose semen is scanty, and who cannot bear the warm embrace of the female. Those who differ from this temperament are called men of middling passion, while those of intense passion are full of desire. In the same way, women are supposed to have the degrees of feeling as specified above.

Lastly, according to time there are three kinds

Above: When the woman places her thighs with her legs doubled upon them by her sides, and thus engages in congress, it is called the position of Indrani, or the wife of Indra, and this is learnt only by practice.

Facing page: When one of two lovers presses forcibly one or both of the thighs between his or her own it is called the 'embrace of thighs'.

of men and women, viz. the short-timed, the moderate-timed, and the long-timed, and of these as in the previous statements, there are nine kinds of union.

But on this last head there is a difference of opinion about the female which should be stated.

Auddalika says, 'Females do not emit as males do. The males simply remove their desire, while the females, from their consciousness of desire, feel a certain kind of pleasure, which gives them satisfaction, but it is impossible for them to tell you what kind of pleasure they feel. The fact from which this becomes evident is that males, when engaged in coition, cease of themselves after emission, and are satisfied, but it is not so with females.'

The opinion is however objected to on the grounds, that if a male be long-timed, the female loves him the more, but if he be short-timed, she is dissatisfied with him. And this circumstance, some say, would prove that the female emits also. But this opinion does not hold good, for if it takes a long time to allay a woman's desire, and during this time she is enjoying great pleasure, it is quite natural then that she should wish for its continuation. And on this subject there is a verse as follows: 'By union with men the lust, desire, or passion of women is satisfied, and the pleasure derived from the consciousness of it is called their satisfaction.'

The followers of Babhravya, however, say that the semen of women continues to fall from the beginning of the sexual union to its end, and it is right that it should be so, for if they had no semen there would be no embryo. To this there is no objection. In the beginning of coition the passion of the woman is middling, and she cannot bear the vigorous thrusts of her lover, but by degrees her passion increases until she ceases to think about her body, and then finally she wishes to stop from further coition.

This objection, however, does not hold good, for even in ordinary things that revolve with great force, such as a potter's wheel, or a top, we find that the motion at first is slow, but by degrees it becomes very rapid. In the same way the passion of the woman having gradually increased, she has a desire to discontinue coition, when all the semen has fallen away. And there is a verse with regard to this as follows: 'The fall of the semen of the man takes place only at the end of coition, while the semen of the woman falls continually, and after the semen of both has all fallen away then they wish for the discontinuance of coition'.

Lastly, Vatsyayana is of the view that the semen of the female falls in the same way as that of the male. Now some may ask here: If men and women are beings of the same kind, and are engaged in bringing about the same result, why should they have different work to do? Vatsyayana says that this is so, because the ways of working, by which men are the actors, and women are the persons acted upon, is owing to the nature of the male and the female, otherwise the actor would be sometimes the person acted upon, and vice versa. And from this difference in the ways of working follows the difference in the consciousness of pleasure, for a man thinks, 'This woman is united with me,' and a woman thinks, 'I am united with this man.'

It may be said that if the ways of working in men and women are different, why should not there be a difference even in the pleasure they feel, and which is the result of those ways.

But this objection is groundless, for the person acting and the person acted upon being of different kinds, there is a reason for the difference in their ways of working; but there is no reason for any difference in the pleasure they feel, because they both naturally derive pleasure from the act they perform.

On this again some may say that when different persons are engaged in doing the same work, we find that they accomplish the same end or purpose; while, on the contrary, in the case of men and women we find that each of them accomplishes his or her own end separately, and this is inconsistent. But this is a mistake, for we find that sometimes two things are done at the same time, as for instance in the fighting of rams, both the rams receive the shock at the same time on their heads. Again, in throwing one wood apple against another, and also in a fight or struggle of wrestlers. If it be said that in these cases the things employed are of the same kind, it is answered that even in the case of men and women, the nature of the two persons is the same. And as the difference in their ways of working arises from the difference of their conformation only, it follows that men experience the same kind of pleasure as women do.

There is also a verse on this subject as follows: 'Men and women being of the same nature, feel the same kind of pleasure, and therefore a man should marry such a woman as will love him ever afterwards.'

The pleasure of men and women thus being proved to be of the same kind, it follows that in regard to time, there are nine kinds of sexual intercourse, in the same way as there are nine kinds of union, according to the force of passion.

There being thus nine kinds of union with regard to dimensions, force of passion, and time, respectively, by making combinations of them, innumerable kinds of union would be produced. Therefore in each particular kind of sexual union, men should use such means as they may think suitable for the occasion.

At the first time of sexual union the passion of the male is intense, and his time is short, but in subsequent unions on the same day the reverse of this is the case. With the female, however, it is the contrary, for at the first time her passion is weak, and then her time short, until her passion is satisfied.

Men learned in the humanities are of the opinion that love is of four kinds:love acquired by continual habit; love resulting from the imagination; love resulting from belief; love resulting from the perception of external objects.

1) Love resulting from the constant and continual performance of some act, is called love acquired by constant practice and habit, as for instance the love of sexual intercourse, the love of hunting, the love of drinking, the love of gambling, etc.

2) Love which is felt for things to which we are not habituated, and which proceeds entirely from ideas, is called love resulting from imagination, as for instance, that love which some men and women and eunuchs feel for the Auparishtaka or mouth congress, and that which is felt by all for such things as embracing, kissing, etc.

3) The love which is mutual on both sides, and proved to be true, when each looks upon the other as his or her very own, such is called love resulting from belief by the learned.

4) The love resulting from the perception of external objects is quite evident and well known to the world, because the pleasure which it affords is superior to the pleasure of the other kinds of love, which exists only for its sake.

What has been said in this chapter upon the subject of sexual union is sufficient for the learned; but for the edification of the ignorant, the same will now be treated of at length and in detail.

V

Of the embrace

This part of the *Kama Shastra*, which treats of sexual union, is called 'Sixty-four', *Chatushshashti*. Some old authors say that it is called so, because it contains sixty-four chapters. Others are of opinion that the author of this part being a person named Panchala, and the person who recited the part of the Rig Veda called Dashatapa, which contains sixty-four verses, being also called Panchala, the name 'sixty-four' has been given to the part of the work in honour of the Rig Vedas. The followers of Babhravya say on the other hand that this part contains eight subjects, viz. the embrace, kissing, scratching with the nails or fingers, biting, lying down, making various sounds, playing the part of the man, and the Auparishtaka or mouth congress. Each of these subjects being of eight kinds, and eight multiplied by eight being sixty-four, this part is therefore named 'sixty-four'. But Vatsyayana affirms that as this part contains also the following subjects, viz. striking, crying, the acts of man during congress, the various kinds of congress, and other subjects, the name 'sixty-four' is given to it only accidentally. As, for instance, we say this tree is 'Saptaparna', or seven-leaved, this offering of rice is 'Panchavarna', or five-coloured, but the tree has not seven leaves, neither has the rice five colours.

However the part sixty-four is now treated of, and the embrace, being the first subject, will now be considered. Now the embrace, which indicates the mutual love of a man and a woman

Above: When a man and a woman are much in love with each other and, not thinking of any pain or hurt, embrace each other as if they were entering into each other's bodies either while the woman is sitting on the lap of the man, or in front of him, or on a bed, then it is called an embrace like 'mixture of milk and water'.

Facing page: It is said by some that there is no fixed time or order between the embrace, the kiss, and the pressing or scratching with the nails or fingers, but that all these things should be done generally before sexual union takes place. . . Vatsyayana however, thinks that anything may take place at any time, for love does not care for time or order.

who have come together is of four kinds viz. touching; piercing; rubbing; pressing. The action in each case is denoted by the meaning of the word which stands for it.

1) When a man under some pretext or other, goes in front or alongside of a woman and touches her body with his own, it is called the 'touching embrace'.

2) When a woman in a lonely place bends down, as if to pick up something, and pierces, as it were, a man sitting or standing, with her breasts, and the man in return takes hold of them, it is called a 'piercing embrace'.

The above two kinds of embrace take place only between persons who do not, as yet, speak freely with each other.

3) When two lovers are walking slowly together, either in the dark, or in a place of public resort, or in a lonely place, and rub their bodies against each other, it is called a 'rubbing embrace'.

4) When on the above occasion one of them presses the other's body forcibly against a wall or pillar, it is called a 'pressing embrace'.

These two last embraces are peculiar to those who know the intentions of each other.

At the time of the meeting, the four following kinds of embrace are used viz. *Jataveshitaka* or the twining of a creeper; *Vrikshadhirudhaka* or climbing a tree; *Til-tandulaka* or the mixture of sesamum seed with rice; *Kshiraniraka* or milk and water embrace.

1) When a woman, clinging to a man as a creeper twines round a tree, bends his head down to hers with the desire of kissing him and embraces him, and looks lovingly towards him, it is called an embrace like the 'twining of a creeper'.

2) When a woman, having placed one of her feet on the foot of her lover, and the other on one of his thighs, passes one of her arms round his back, and the other on his shoulders, makes slightly the sounds of singing and cooing, and wishes, as it were, to climb up to him in order to have a kiss, it is called an embrace like the' climbing of a tree'.

These two kinds of embrace take place when the lover is standing.

3) When lovers lie on a bed, and embrace each other so closely that the arms and thighs of the one are encircled by the arms and thighs of the other, and, are, as it were, rubbing up against them, this is called an embrace like the 'mixture of sesamum seed with rice'.

4) When a man and a woman are much in love with each other and, not thinking of any pain or hurt, embrace each other as if they were entering into each other's bodies either while the woman is sitting on the lap of the man, or in front of him, or on a bed, then it is called an embrace like a' mixture of milk and water'.

These two kinds of embrace take place at the time of sexual union.

Babhravya has thus related to us the above eight kinds of embraces.

Suvarnanabha moreover gives us four ways of embracing simple members of the body, which are: the embrace of the thighs; the embrace of the *jaghana* i.e. the part of the body from the navel downwards to the thighs; the embrace of the breasts; the embrace of the forehead.

1) When one of two lovers presses forcibly one or both of the thighs of the other between his or her own it is called the 'embrace of thighs'.

2) When a man presses the *jaghana* or middle part of the woman's body against his own, and mounts upon her to practice, either scratching with the nail or finger, or biting, or striking, or kissing, the hair of the woman being loose and flowing, it is called the 'embrace of the *jaghana*'.

3) When a man places his breast between the breasts of a woman and presses her with it, it is called the 'embrace of the breasts'.

4) When either of the lovers touches the mouth, the eyes and the forehead of the other with his or her own, it is called the 'embrace of the forehead'.

Some say that even shampooing is a kind of embrace, because there is a touching of bodies in it. But Vatsyayana thinks that as shampooing is performed at a different time, and for a different purpose, and it is also of a different character, it cannot be said to be included in the embrace.

There are also some verses on the subject as follows; 'The whole subject of embracing is of such a nature that men who ask questions about it, or who hear about it, or who talk about it, acquire thereby a desire for enjoyment. Even those embraces that are not mentioned in the *Kama Shastra* should be practised at the time of sexual enjoyment, if they are in any way conducive to the increase of love or passion. The rules of the *Shastra* apply so long as the passion of man is middling, but when the wheel of love is once set in motion, there is then no *Shastra* and no order.'

VI

Of kissing

It is said by some that there is no fixed time or order between the embrace, the kiss, and the pressing or scratching with the nails or fingers, but that all these things should be done generally before sexual union takes place, while striking and making the various sounds generally takes place at the time of the union. Vatsyayana however, thinks that anything may take place at any time, for love does not care for time or order.

On the occasion of the first congress, kissing and the other things mentioned above should be done moderately, they should not be continued for a long time, and should be done alternately. On subsequent occasions however the reverse of all this may take place, and moderation will not be necessary, they may continue for a long time, and for the purpose of kindling love, they may be all done at the same time.

The following are the places for kissing - the forehead, the eyes, the cheeks, the throat, the bosom, the breasts, the lips, and the interior of the mouth. In case of a young girl, there are three sorts of kisses; the nominal kiss; the throbbing kiss; the touching kiss.

1) When a girl only touches the mouth of her lover with her own, but does not herself do anything, it is called the 'nominal kiss'.

2) When a girl, setting aside her bashfulness a little, wishes to touch the lip that is pressed into her mouth, and with that object moves her lower lip, but not the upper one, it is called the 'throbbing kiss'.

3) When a girl touches her lover's lip with her tongue, and having shut her eyes, places her hands on those of her lover, it is called the 'touching kiss'.

Other authors describe four other kinds of kisses: the straight kiss; the bent kiss; the turned kiss; the pressed kiss.

1) When the lips of two lovers are brought into direct contact with each other, it is called a 'straight kiss'.

2) When the heads of two lovers are bent towards each other, and when so bent, kissing takes place, it is called a 'bent kiss'.

3) When one of them turns up the face of the other by holding the head and chin, and then kissing, it is called a 'turned kiss'.

4) Lastly when the lower lip is pressed with much force, it is called a 'pressed kiss'.

There is also a fifth kind of kiss called the 'greatly pressed kiss', which is effected by taking hold of the lower lip between two fingers, and then after touching it with the tongue, pressing it with great force with the lip.

As regards kissing, a wager may be laid as to which will get hold of the other first. If the woman loses, she should pretend to cry, should keep her lover off by shaking her hands, and turn away from him and dispute with him saying, 'Let another wager be laid.' If she loses this a second time, she should appear doubly distressed, and when her lover is off his guard or asleep, she should get hold of his lower lip, and hold it in her teeth, so that it should not slip away, and then she should laugh, make a loud noise, deride him, dance about, and say whatever she likes in a joking way, moving her eyebrows, and rolling her eyes. Such are the wagers and quarrels as far as kissing is concerned, but the same may be applied with regard to the pressing or scratching with the nails and fingers, biting and striking. All these however, are only peculiar to men and women of intense passion.

When a man kisses the upper lip of a woman, while she in return kisses his lower lip, it is called 'the kiss of the upper lip'.

When one of them takes both the lips of the other between his or her own, it is called a 'clasping kiss'. A woman, however, only takes this kind of kiss from a man who has no moustache. And on the occasion of the kiss, if one of them

Above: Even those embraces that are not mentioned in the *Kama Shastra* should be practised at the time of sexual enjoyment, if they are in any way conducive to the increase of love or passion. The rules of the *Shastra* apply so long as the passion of man is middling, but when the wheel of love is once set in motion, then there is no *Shastra* and no order.

Facing page: On the occasion of the first congress, kissing should be done moderately, and should not be continued for a long time. . . when one of two lovers turns up the face of the other by holding the head and chin, and then kissing, it is called a 'turned kiss'.

touches the teeth, the tongue, and the palate of the other, with his or her tongue, it is called the 'fighting of the tongues'. In the same way, the pressing of the teeth of the one against the mouth of the other is to be practised.

Kissing is of four kinds, viz. moderate, contracted, pressed and soft, according to the different parts of the body that are kissed, for different kinds of kisses are appropriate for different parts of the body.

When a woman looks at the face of her lover while he is asleep, and kisses it to show her intention or desire, it is called a 'kiss that kindles love'.

When a woman kisses her lover while he is engaged in business, or while he is quarrelling with her, or while he is looking at something else, so that his mind may be turned away, it is called a 'kiss that turns away'.

When a lover coming home late at night kisses his beloved, who is asleep on her bed, in order to show her his desire, it is called a 'kiss that awakens'. On such an occasion the woman may pretend to be asleep at the time of her lover's arrival, so that she may know his intention and obtain respect from him.

When a person kisses the reflection of the person he loves in a mirror, in water, or on a wall, it is called a 'kiss showing the intention'.

When a person kisses a child sitting on his lap, or a picture, or an image, or figure, in the presence of the person beloved by him, it is called a 'transferred kiss'.

When at night at a theatre, or in an assembly of caste men, a man coming up to a woman kisses a finger of her hand if she be standing, or a toe of her foot if she be sitting, or when a woman is shampooing her lover's body, places her face on his thigh, (as if she was sleepy) so as to inflame his passion, and kisses his thigh or great toe, it is called a 'demonstrative kiss'.

Whatever things may be done by one of the lovers to the other, the same should be returned by the other i.e. if the woman kisses him he should kiss her in return, if she strikes him he should also strike her in return.

VII

Of pressing, or marking, or scratching with the nails

When love becomes intense, pressing with the nails or scratching the body with them is practised, and it is done on the following occasions: on the first visit; at the time of setting out on a journey; on the return from a journey; at the time when an angry lover is reconciled; and lastly, when a woman is intoxicated. But pressing with the nails is not a usual thing except with those who are intensely passionate. It is employed together with biting, by those to whom the practice is agreeable.

Pressing with the nails is of the eight following kinds, according to the forms of the marks which are produced: sounding; half moon; a circle; a line; a tiger's nail or claw; a peacock's foot; the jump of a hare; the leaf of a blue lotus.

The places that are to be pressed with the nails are as follows: the armpit, the throat, the breasts, the lips, the *jaghana* or middle parts of the body, and the thighs. The qualities of good nails are that they should be bright, well set, clean, entire, convex, soft, and glossy in appearance.

1) When a person presses the chin, the breasts, the lower lip, or the *jaghana* of another so softly that no scratch or mark is left, but only the hair on the body becomes erect from the touch of the nails, and the nails themselves make a sound, it is called a 'sounding or pressing with the nails'. This pressing is used in the case of a young girl when her lover shampoos her, scratches her head, and wants to trouble or frighten her.

2) The curved mark with the nails, which is impressed on the neck and the breasts, is called 'the half moon'.

3) When the half moons are impressed opposite to each other, it is called a 'circle'. This mark with the nails is generally made on the navel, the small cavities about the buttocks, and on the joint of the thigh.

4) A mark in the form of a small line, and which can be made on any part of the body, is called a 'line'.

5) This same line, when it is curved, and

made on the breast, is called a 'tiger's nail'.

6) When a curved mark is made on the breast by means of the five nails, it is called a 'peacock's foot'. This mark is made with the object of being praised, for it requires a great deal of skill to make it properly.

7) When five marks with the nails are made close to one another near the nipple of the breast, it is called 'the jump of a hare'.

8) A mark made on the breast or on the hips in the form of a leaf of the blue lotus, is called the 'leaf of a blue lotus'.

When a person is going on a journey, and makes a mark on the thighs, or on the breast, it is called a 'token of remembrance'. On such an occasion three or four lines are impressed close to one another with the nails. Marks of other kinds than the above may also be made with the nails, for the ancient authors say, that as there are innumerable degrees of skill among men (the practice of this art being known to all), so there are innumerable ways of making these marks. And as pressing or marking with the nails is independent of love, no one can say with certainty how many different kinds of marks with the nails do actually exist. The reason for this is, Vatsyayana says, that as variety is necessary in love, so love is to be produced by means of variety. It is on this account that courtesans, who are well acquainted with various ways and means, become so desirable, for if variety is sought in all the arts and amusements, such as archery and others, how much more should it be sought after in the present case.

The marks of the nails should not be made on married women, but particular kinds of marks may be made on their private parts for the remembrance and increase of love.

The love of a woman who sees the marks of nails on the private parts of her body, even th ough they are old and almost worn out, becomes again fresh and new. If there be no marks of nails to remind a person of the passages of love, then love is lessened in the same way as when no union takes place for a long time. Even when a stranger sees at a distance, a young woman with the marks of nails on her breast, he is filled with love and respect for her.

A man, also, who carries the marks of nails and teeth on some parts of his body, influences the mind of a woman, even though it be ever so firm. In short, nothing tends to increase love so much as the effects of marking with the nails, and biting.

VIII

Of the various modes of striking, and appropriate sounds

Sexual intercourse can be compared to a quarrel, on account of the contrarities of love and its tendency to dispute. The place of striking with passion is the body, and on the body the special places are: the shoulders; the head; the space between the breasts; the back; the *jaghana* or middle part of the body; the sides. Striking is of four kinds: striking with back of the hand; striking with the fingers a little contracted; striking with the fist; striking with the open palm of the hand.

On account of its causing pain, striking gives rise to the hissing sound, which is of various kinds, and to the eight kinds of crying, viz. the sound of Hin; the thundering sound; the cooing sound; the weeping sound; the sound Phut; the sound Phat; the sound Sut; the sound Plat.

Besides these, there are also words having a meaning, such as 'mother', and those that are expressive of prohibition, sufficiency, desire of liberation, pain or praise, and to which may be added sounds like those of the dove, the cuckoo, the green pigeon, the parrot, the bee, the sparrow, the flamingo, the duck, and the quail, which are all occasionally made use of.

Blows with the fist should be given on the back of the woman, while she is sitting on the lap of the man, and she should give blows in return, abusing the man as if she were angry, and making the cooing and weeping sounds. While the woman is engaged in congress, the space between the breasts should be struck with the back of the hand, slowly at first, and then proportionately to the increasing excitement, until the end.

At this time, the sound Hin and others may

Facing page and above: Such passionate actions and amorous gesticulations or movements, which arise on the spur of the moment, and during sexual intercourse, cannot be defined. . . a loving pair become blind with passion in the heat of congress, and go on with great impetuosity, paying not the least regard to excess.

be made, alternately or optionally, according to habit. When the man, making the sound Phat, strikes the woman on the head, with the fingers of his hand a little contracted, it is called Prasritaka. In this case, the appropriate sounds are the cooing sound, the sound Phat, and the sound Phut of the interior in the mouth, and at the end of congress, the sighing and weeping sounds. The sound Phat is an imitation of the sound of a bamboo being split, while the sound Phut is like the sound made by something falling into water. At all times, when kissing and such like things are begun, the woman should give a reply with a hissing sound. During the excitement when the woman is not accustomed to striking, she continually utters words expressive of prohibition, sufficiency, or desire of liberation, as well as the words 'father', 'mother', intermingled with the sighing, weeping and thundering sounds. Towards the conclusion of the congress, the breasts, the *jaghana*, and the sides of the woman should be pressed with the open palms of the hand, with some force, until the end of it, and then sounds like those of the quail, or the goose should be made.

There are also two verses on the subject as follows: 'The characteristics of manhood are said to consist of roughness and impetuosity, while weakness, tenderness, sensibility, and an inclination to turn away from unpleasant things are the distinguishing marks of womanhood. The excitement of passion, and pecularities of habit may sometimes cause contrary results to appear, but these do not last long, and in the end the natural state is resumed.'

The wedge on the bosom, the scissors on the head, the piercing instrument on the cheeks, and the pincers on the breasts and sides, may also taken into consideration with the other four modes of striking, and thus give eight ways al-

together. But these four ways of striking with instruments are peculiar to the people of the southern countries, and the marks caused by them are seen on the breasts of their women. They are local peculiarities, but Vatsyayana is of the opinion that the practice of them is painful, barbarous and base, and quite unworthy of imitation.

In the same way, anything that is a local peculiarity should not always be adopted elsewhere, and even in the place where the practice is prevalent, excess of it should always be avoided. Instances of the dangerous use of them may be given as follows. The king of the Panchalas killed the courtesan Madhavasena, by means of the wedge during congress. King Shatakarni Shatavahana of Kuntalas deprived his great Queen Malayavati of her life by a pair of scissors, and Naradeva, whose hand was deformed, blinded a dancing girl by directing a piercing instrument in a wrong way.

Such passionate actions and amorous gesticulations or movements, which arise on the spur of the moment, and during sexual intercourse, cannot be defined, and are as irregular as dreams. A horse, having once attained the fifth degree of motion goes on with blind speed, regardless of pits, ditches, and posts in his way; and in the same manner a loving pair become blind with passion in the heat of congress, and go on with great impetuosity, applying not the least regard to excess. For this reason, one who is well acquainted with the science of love, and knowing his own strength, as also the tenderness, impetuosity, and strength of the young women, should act accordingly. The various modes of enjoyment are not for all times or for all persons, but they should only be used at the proper time, and in the proper countries and places.

IX

Of biting

All the places that can be kissed, are also the places that can be bitten, except the upper lip, the interior of the mouth, and the eyes. The qualities of good teeth are as follows: they should be equal, possessed of a pleasing bright-

ness, capable of being coloured, of proper proportions, unbroken, and with sharp ends.

The defects of teeth on the other hand, are that they are blunt, protruding from the gums, rough, soft, large, and loosely set.

The following are the different kinds of biting: the hidden bite; the swollen bite; the point; the line of points; the coral and the jewel; the line of jewels; the broken cloud; the biting of the boar.

1) The biting which is shown only by the excessive redness of the skin that is bitten, is called the 'hidden bite'.

2) When the skin is pressed down on both sides, it is called the 'swollen bite'.

3) When a small portion of the skin is bitten with two teeth only, it is called the 'point'.

4) When such small portions of the skin are bitten with all the teeth, it is called the 'line of points'.

5) The biting done by bringing together the teeth and the lips, is called the 'coral and the jewel'. The lip is the coral, and the teeth the jewel.

6) When biting is done by all the teeth, it is called the 'line of jewels'.

7) The biting which consists of unequal rising in a circle, and which comes from the space between teeth, is called the 'broken cloud'. This is impressed on the breasts.

8) The biting which consists of many broad rows of marks near to one another, and with red intervals, is called the 'biting of a boar'. This is impressed on the breasts and the shoulders; and these two last modes of biting are peculiar to persons of intense passion.

The lower lip is the place on which the 'hidden bite', the 'swollen bite' and the 'point' are made; again, the 'swollen bite' and the 'coral and the jewel' bite are done on the cheek. Kissing, pressing with the nail, and biting are the ornaments of the left cheek, and when the word cheek is used it is to be understood as the left cheek. Both the 'line of points' and the 'line of jewels' are to be impressed on the throat, the armpit, and the joints of the thighs; but the 'line of point' alone is to be impressed on the forehead and the thighs.

The marking with the nails, and the biting of the following things viz. an ornament of the forehead, an ear ornament, a bunch of flowers, a betel leaf, or a tamala leaf, which are worn by or belong to the woman that is beloved, are signs of the desire of enjoyment. Among the things mentioned above viz. embracing, kissing, etc. those which increase passion should be done first, and those which are only for amusement or variety should be done afterwards.

There are also some verses on this subject as follows: 'When a man bites a woman forcibly, she should angrily do the same to him with double force. Thus a 'point' should be returned with a 'line of points', and a 'line of points' with a 'broken cloud', and if she be excessively chafed, she should at once begin a love quarrel with him. At such a time she should take hold of her lover by the hair, and bend his head down, and kiss his lower lip, and then, being intoxicated with love, she should shut her eyes and bite him in various places. Even by day, and in a place of public resort, when her lover shows her any mark that she may have inflicted on his body, she should smile at the sight of it, and turning her face as if she were going to chide him, she should show him with angry look the marks on her own body that have been made by him. Thus, if men and women act according to each other's liking, their love for each other will not be lessened even in one hundred years.'

X

Of the various kinds of congress

On the occasion of 'high congress' the Mrigi (Deer) woman should lie down in such a way as to widen her *yoni*, while in a 'low congress' the Hastini (Elephant) woman should lie down so as to contract hers. But in an 'equal congress' they should lie down in the natural position. What is said above concerning the Mrigi and the Hastini, applies also to the Vadawa (Mare) woman. In a 'low congress' the woman should particularly make use of medicine, to cause her desire to be satisfied quickly.

The Deer woman has the following three ways of lying down: the widely opened position; the yawning position; the position of the wife of Indra.

1) When she lowers her head and raises her

Above: Desire which springs from nature, and which is increased by art, and from which all danger is taken away by wisdom, becomes firm and secure. A clever man, depending on his own ability, and observing carefully the ideas and thoughts of women, and removing the causes of their turning away from men, is generally successful with them.

Facing page: When a man is trying to gain over a woman, he should examine the state of her mind, and then act. . . when a woman gives a man an opportunity, and makes her own love manifest to him, he should proceed to enjoy her.

middle parts, it is called the 'widely opened position'. At such a time, the man should apply some unguent, so as to make the entrance easy.

2) When she raises her thighs and keeps them wide apart and engages in congress, it is called the 'yawning position'.

3) When she places her thighs with her legs doubled on them upon her sides, and thus engages in congress, it is called the position of Indrani, and this is learnt only by practice. The position is also useful in the case of the 'highest congress'.

The 'clasping position' is used in 'low congress', and in the 'lowest congress', together with the 'pressing position', the 'twining position', and the 'mare's position'.

When the legs of both the male and the female are stretched straight out over each other, it is called the 'clasping position'. It is of two kinds, the side position and the supine position, according to the way in which they lie down. In the side position, the male should invariably lie on his left side, and cause the woman to lie on her right side, and this rule is to be observed in lying down with all kinds of women.

When, after congress has begun in the clasping position, the woman presses her lover with her thighs, it is called the 'pressing position'.

When the woman places one of her thighs across the thigh of her lover, it is called the 'twining position'.

When a woman forcibly holds the *lingam* in her *yoni* after it is in, it is called the 'mare's position'. This is learnt by practice only.

The above are the different ways of lying down, mentioned by Babhravya; Suvarnanabha, however, gives the following in addition.

When the female raises both of her thighs straight up, it is called the 'raising position'.

When she raises both of her legs, and places them on her lover's shoulders, it is called the 'yawning position'.

When the legs are contracted, and thus held by the lover before his bosom, it is called the 'pressed position'.

When only one of her legs is stretched out, it is called the 'half pressed position'.

When the woman places one of her legs on her lover's shoulder, and stretches the other out, and then places the latter on his shoulder, and stretches out the other and continues to do so alternately, it is called the 'splitting of a bamboo'.

When one of her legs is placed on the head, and the other is stretched out, it is called the 'fixing of a nail'. This is learnt by practice only.

When both the legs of the woman are contracted, and placed on her stomach, it is called the 'crab's position'.

When the thighs are raised and placed one upon the other, it is called the 'packed position'.

When the shanks are placed one upon the other, it is called the 'lotus-like position'.

When a man, during congress, turns round, and enjoys the woman without leaving her, while she embraces him round the back all the time, it is called the 'turning position', and is learnt only by practice.

Thus says Suvarnanabha, these different ways of lying down, sitting, and standing should be practised in water because it is easy to do therein. But Vatsyayana is of the view that congress in water is improper, because it is prohibited by the religious law.

When a man and a woman support themselves on each other's bodies, or on a wall, or pillar, and thus while standing engage in congress, it is called the 'supported congress'.

When a man supports himself against a wall, and the woman, sitting on his hands joined together and held underneath her, throws her arms round his neck, and putting her thighs alongside his waist, moves herself by her feet, which are touching the wall against which the man is leaning, it is called the 'suspended congress'.

When a woman stands on her hands and feet like a quadruped, and her lover mounts her like a bull, it is called the 'congress of a cow'. At this time, everything that is ordinarily done on the bosom should be done on the back. In the same way can be carried on the congress of a dog, the congress of a goat, the congress of a deer, the forcible mounting of an ass, the congress of a cat, the jump of a tiger, the pressing of an elephant, the rubbing of a boar, and the mounting of a horse. And in all these cases the characteristics of these different animals should be manifested by acting like them.

When a man enjoys two women at the same time, both of whom love him equally, it is called the 'united congress'.

When a man enjoys many women altogether,

it is called the 'congress of a herd of cows'.

The following kinds of congress viz. sporting in water, or the congress of an elephant with many female elephants which is said to take place only in the water, the congress of a collection of goats, the congress of a collection of deer, take place in imitation of these animals.

In Gramaneri, many young men enjoy a woman, who may be married to one of them, either one after the other, or at the same time. Thus, one of them holds her, another enjoys her, a third uses her mouth, a fourth holds her middle part, and in this way they go on enjoying her several parts alternately. The same things can be done when several men are sitting in company with one courtesan, or when one courtesan is alone with many men. In the same way this can be done by the women of the king's harem, when they accidentally get hold of a man.

The people in the southern countries have also a congress in the anus, that is called the 'lower congress'.

Thus end the various kinds of congress. There are two verses on the subject as follows: 'An ingenious person should multiply the kinds of congress after the fashion of the different kinds of beasts and of birds. For these different kinds of congress, performed according to the usage of each country, and the liking of each individual, generate love, friendship, and respect in the hearts of women.'

XI

Of role reversal

When a woman sees that her lover is fatigued by constant congress, without having his desire satisfied, she should, with his permission, lay him down upon his back, and give him assistance by acting his part. She may also do this to satisfy the curiosity of her lover, or her own desire of novelty.

There are two ways of doing this. The first is when during congress she turns round, and gets on the top of her lover, in such a manner as to continue the congress, without obstructing the pleasure of it; and the other is when she acts the man's part from the beginning. At such a time, with her hair hanging loose, and her smiles broken by hard breathing, she should press upon her lover's bosom with her own breasts, and lowering her head frequently, should do in return the same actions which he used to do before, returning his blows, and chaffing him, should say, 'I was laid down by you, and fatigued with hard congress. I shall now therefore lay you down in return.' She should then again manifest her own bashfulness, her fatigue, and her desire for stopping the congress.

Whatever is done by a man for giving pleasure to a woman is called the work of a man, and is as follows: While the woman is lying on his bed, and is as it were, abstracted by his conversation, he should loosen the knot of her undergarments, and when she begins to dispute with him, he should overwhelm her with kisses. Then when his *lingam* is erect, he should touch her with his hands in various places, and gently manipulate various parts of the body. If the woman is bashful, and if it is the first time that they have come together, the man should place his hands between her thighs, which she would probably keep close together, and if she is a very young girl, he should first get his hand upon her breast, which she would probably cover with her own hands, and under her armpits and on her neck. If, however, she is a seasoned woman, he should do whatever is agreeable either to him or to her, and whatever is fitting for the occasion. After this he should take hold of her hair, and hold her chin in his fingers for the purpose of kissing her. On this, if she is a young girl, she will become bashful and close her eyes. Anyhow he should gather from the action of the woman, what things would be pleasing to her during congress.

The signs of the enjoyment and satisfaction of the woman are as follows: her body relaxes, she closes her eyes, she puts aside all bashfulness, and shows increased willingness to unite the two organs as closely together as possible. On the other hand, the signs of her want of enjoyment and of failing to be satisfied are as follows:

Above: . . . with her hair hanging loose,and her smiles broken by hard breathing, she should press upon her lover's bosom with her own breasts, and lowering her head frequently, should do in return the same actions which he used to do before, returning his blows, and chaffing him, should say, 'I was laid down by you, and fatigued with hard congress. I shall now therefore lay you down in return'.

Facing page: When a woman sees that her lover is fatigued by constant congress, without having his desire satisfied, she should, with his permission, lay him down upon his back, and give him assistance by acting his part. She may also do this to satisfy the curiosity of her lover, or her own desire of novelty.

she shakes her hands, she does not let the man get up, feels dejected, bites the man, kicks him, and continues to go on moving after the man has finished. In such cases, the man should rub the *yoni* of the woman with his hand and fingers (as the elephant rubs anything with his trunk) before engaging in congress, until it is softened, and after that is done he should proceed to put his *lingam* into her.

The acts to be done by the man are: moving forward; friction or churning; piercing; rubbing; pressing; giving a blow; the blow of a boar; the blow of a bull; the sporting of a sparrow.

1) When the organs are brought together properly and directly it is called 'moving the organ forward'.

2) When the *lingam* is held with the hand, and turned all round in the *yoni*, it is called 'churning'.

3) When the *yoni* is lowered, and the upper part of it is struck with the *lingam*, it is called 'piercing'.

4) When the same thing is done on the lower part of the *yoni*, it is called 'rubbing'.

5) When the *yoni* is pressed by the *lingam* for a long time, it is called 'pressing'.

6) When the *lingam* is removed to some distance from the *yoni*, and then forcibly strikes it, it is called 'giving a blow'.

7) When only one part of the *yoni* is rubbed with the *lingam*, it is called the 'blow of a boar'.

8) When both sides of the *yoni* are rubbed in this way, it is called the 'blow of a bull'.

9) When the *lingam* is in the *yoni*, and moved up and down frequently, and without being taken out, it is called the 'sporting of a sparrow'. This takes place at the end of the congress.

When a woman acts the part of a man, she has the following things to do in addition to the nine given above viz. the pair of tongs; the top; the swing.

1) When the woman holds the *lingam* in her *yoni*, draws it in, presses it, and keeps it thus in her for a long time, it is called the 'pair of tongs'.

2) When, while engaged in congress, she turns round like a wheel, it is called the 'top'. This is learnt by practice only.

3) When, on such an occasion, the man lifts up the middle part of the body, and the woman turns round her middle part, it is called the 'swing'.

When the woman is tired, she should place her forehead on that of her lover, and should thus take rest without disturbing the union of the organs, and when the woman has rested herself, the man should turn round and begin the congress again.

There are also some verses on the subject as follows: 'Though a woman is reserved, and keeps her feelings concealed, yet when she gets on the top of a man, she then shows all her love and desire. A man should gather from the actions of the woman of what disposition she is, and in what way she likes to be enjoyed. A woman during her monthly courses, a woman who has been lately confined, and a fat woman should not be made to act the part of a man.

XII

Of the Auparishtaka or mouth congress

There are two kinds of eunuchs, those that are disguised as males, and those that are disguised as females. Eunuchs disguised as females, imitate their dress, speech, gestures, tenderness, timidity, simplicity, softness and bashfulness. The acts that are done on the *jaghana* or middle parts of women, are done in the mouth of these eunuchs, and this is called Auparishtaka. These eunuchs derive their imaginable pleasure, and their livelihood from this kind of congress, and they lead the life of courtesans. So much concerning eunuchs disguised as females.

Eunuchs disguised as males, keep their desires secret, and when they wish to do anything they lead the life of shampooers. Under the pretence of shampooing, an eunuch of this kind embraces and draws towards himself, the thighs of the man whom he is shampooing, and after this he touches the joints of the thighs and his *jaghana*, or central portions of his body. Then, if he finds the *lingam* of the man erect, he presses it with his hands, and chaffs him for getting into that stage. If after this, and after knowing his intention, the man does not tell the eunuch to proceed, then the latter does it of his own accord and begins the congress. If however, he is ordered by the man to do it, then he disputes with him, and only consents at last with difficulty.

The following eight things are then done by the eunuch, one after the other viz. the nominal congress; biting the sides; pressing outside; pressing inside; kissing; rubbing; sucking a mango fruit; swallowing up.

At the end of each of these, the eunuch expresses his wish to stop, but when one of them is finished, the man desires him to do another, and after that is done, then the one that follows it, and so on.

1) When, holding the man's *lingam* with his hand, and placing it between his lips, the eunuch moves his mouth about, it is called the 'nominal congress'.

2) When, covering the end of the *lingam* with his fingers collected together like the bud of a plant or a flower, the eunuch presses the sides of it with the lips, using his teeth also, it is called 'biting the sides'.

3) When, being desired to proceed, the eunuch presses the end of the *lingam* with his lips closed together, and kisses it as if he were drawing it out, it is called the 'outside pressing'.

4) When, being asked to go on, he puts the *lingam* further into his mouth, and presses it with his lips and then takes it out, it is called the 'inside pressing'.

5) When, holding the *lingam* in his hand, the eunuch kisses it as if he were kissing the lower part, it is called 'kissing'.

6) When, after kissing it, he touches it with his tongue everywhere, and passes the tongue over the end of it, it is called 'rubbing'.

7) When, in the same way, he puts the half of it into his mouth, and forcibly kisses and sucks it, this is called 'sucking a mango fruit'.

8) And lastly, when, with the consent of the man, the eunuch puts the whole *lingam* into his mouth, and presses it to the very end, it is called 'swallowing up'.

Striking, scratching, and other things may also be done during this kind of congress.

The Auparishtaka is practised also by unchaste and wanton women, female attendants and serving maids i.e. those who are not married to anybody, but who live by shampooing.

The Acharyas (i.e. ancient and venerable authors) are of the opinion that this Auparishtaka is the work of a dog and not a man, because it is a low practice, and opposed to the orders of the Holy Writ, and because the man himself suffers by bringing his *lingam* into contact with the mouth of eunuchs and women. But Vatsyayana says that the orders of the Holy Writ do not affect those who resort to courtesans, and the law only prohibits the practice of the Auparishtaka with married women. As regards the injury to the male, that can be easily remedied.

The male servants of some men carry on the mouth congress with their masters. It is also practised by some citizens who know each other well, among themselves. Some women of the harem, when they are amorous, do the acts of the mouth on the *yonis* of one another, and some men do the same thing with women. The way of doing this (i.e. of kissing the *yoni*) should be known from kissing the mouth. When a man and woman lie down in an inverted order i.e. with the head of the one towards the feet of the other, and carry on this congress, it is called the 'congress of crow'.

For the sake of such things, courtesans abandon men possessed of good qualities, liberal and clever, and become attached to low persons, such as slaves and elephant drivers. The Auparishtaka, or mouth congress, should never be done by a learned Brahman, by a minister that carries on the business of a state, or by a man of good reputation, because though the practice is allowed by the Shastras, there is no reason why it should be carried on, and need only be practiced in particular cases. As for instance, the taste, and the strength, and digestive qualities of the flesh of dogs are mentioned in works on medicine, but it does not therefore follow, that it should be eaten by the wise. In the same way, there are some men, some places and some times, with respect to which these practices can be made use of. A man should therefore pay regard to the place, to the time, and to the practice which is to be carried out, as also as to whether it is agreeable to his nature and to himself, and then he may or may not practice

Above: A man who has seen and perceived the feeling of the girl towards him, and who has noticed the outward signs and movements by which these feelings are expressed, should do everything in his power to effect a union with her. He should gain over a young girl by childlike sports, a damsel come-of-age by his skill in the arts, and a girl that loves him by having recourse to persons in whom she confides.

Facing page: In Gramaneri, many young men enjoy a woman, who may be married to one of them, either one after the other, or at the same time. Thus, one of them holds her, another enjoys her, a third uses her mouth, a fourth holds her middle part, and in this way they go on enjoying her several parts alternately.

these things according to circumstances. But after all, these things being done secretly, and the mind of the man being fickle, how can it be known what any person will do at any particular time and for any particular purpose?

XIII

Of the ways of exciting desire

If a man is unable to satisfy a Hastini, or elephant woman, he should have recourse to various means to excite her passion. At the commencement he should rub her *yoni* with his hand or fingers, and not begin to have intercourse with her until she becomes excited or experiences pleasure. This is one way of exciting a woman. Or, he may make use of certain Apadravyas, or things which are put on or around the *lingam* to supplement its length or its thickness, so as to fit it to the *yoni*. In the opinion of Babhravya, these Apadravyas should be made of gold, silver, copper, iron, ivory, buffalo's horn, various kinds of woods, tin or lead, and should be soft, cool, provocative of sexual vigour, and well fitted to serve the intended purpose. Vatsyayana, however, says that they may be made according to the natural liking of each individual.

The following are the different kind of Apadravyas: the 'armlet' (Valaya) should be of the same size as the *lingam*, and should have its outer surface made rough with globules; the 'couple' (Sanghati) is formed of two armlets; the 'bracelet' (Chudaka) is made by joining three or more armlets, until they come up to the required length of the *lingam*; the 'single bracelet' is formed by wrapping a single wire around the *lingam*, according to its dimensions; the Kantuka or Jalaka is a tube open at both ends, outwardly rough and studded with soft globules, and made to fit the side of the *yoni*, and tied to the waist.

When such a thing cannot be obtained, then a tube made of the wood apple, or tubular stalk of the bottle gourd, or a reed made soft with oil and extracts of plants, and tied to the waist with strings may be made use of, as also a row of soft pieces of wood tied together.

The above are the things that can be used in connection with or in the place of the *lingam*.

There are also some verses in conclusion: 'He who is acquainted with the true principles of this science of love pays regard to *Dharma, Artha, Kama*, and to his own experiences, as well as to the teachings of others, and does not act simply on the dictates of his own desire. As for the errors in the science which I have mentioned in this work, on my own authority as an author, I have, immediately after mentioning them, carefully censured and prohibited them.'

'An act is never looked upon with indulgence for the simple reason that it is authorised by the science, because it ought to be remembered that it is the intention of the science, that the rules which it contains should only be acted upon in particular cases. After reading and considering the works of Babhravya and other ancient authors, and thinking over the meaning of the rules given by them, the *Kama Sutra* was composed, according to the precepts of the Holy Writ, for the benefit of the world, by Vatsyayana, while leading the life of a religious student, and wholly engaged in the contemplation of the Deity.'

'This work is not intended to be used merely as an instrument for satisfying our desires. A person acquainted with the true principles of this science, and who preserves his *Dharma, Artha*, and *Kama*, and has regard for the practices of the people, is sure to obtain the mastery over his senses.'

'In short, an intelligent and prudent person, attending to *Dharma* and *Artha* and attending to *Kama* also, without becoming the slave of his passions, obtains success in everything that he may undertake.'

Part

II

On Seduction

I

Of the characteristics of men and women

A man may resort to the wife of another, for the purpose of saving his own life, when he perceives that his love for her proceeds from one degree of intensity to another. These degrees are ten in number, and are distinguished by the following marks: love of the eye; attachment of the mind; constant reflection, destruction of sleep; emaciation of the body; turning away from objects of enjoyment; removal of shame; madness; fainting; death.

Ancient authors say that a man should know the disposition, truthfulness, purity and will of a young woman, as also the intensity or weakness of her passions, from the form of her body, and from her characteristic marks and signs. But Vatsyayana is of the view that the forms of bodies, and the characteristic marks or signs are but erring tests of character, and that women should be judged by their conduct, by the outward expression of their thoughts, and by the movements of their bodies.

Now as a general rule, Gonikaputra says that a woman falls in love with every handsome man she sees, and frequently does not take any other steps, owing to various considerations. In love the following circumstances are peculiar to the woman. She loves without regard to right or wrong, and does not try to gain over a man simply for the attainment of some particular purpose. Moreover, when a man first makes up to her, she appears unwilling to unite herself with him. But when the attempts to gain her are repeated and renewed, she at last consents. But with a man, even though he may have begun to love, he conquers his feelings from a regard for morality and wisdom, and although his thoughts are often on the woman, he does not yield, even though an attempt be made to gain him over. He sometimes makes an attempt or effort to win the object of his affections, and having failed, he leaves her alone for the future. In the same way, when a woman is once gained, he often becomes indifferent about her.

The causes of a woman rejecting the addresses of a man are as follows: affection for her husband; desire of lawful progeny; want of certainty on account of the man being devoted to travelling; thinking that the man may be attached to some other person; fear of the man's not keeping his intentions secret; thinking that the man is too devoted to his friends, and has too great a regard for them; the apprehension that he is not in earnest; bashfulness on account of his being an illustrious man; fear on account of his being powerful, or possessed of too impetuous passion, in the case of the deer woman; bashfulness on account of his being too clever; the thought of having once lived with him only on friendly terms; contempt of his want of knowledge of the world; distrust of his low character; disgust at his want of perception of her

Above: In the beginning of coition the passion of the woman is middling, and she cannot bear the vigorous thrusts of her lover, but by degrees her passion increases until she ceases to think about her body.

Facing page: Now a girl always shows her love by outward signs and actions, such as the following: she never looks the man in the face, and becomes abashed when she is looked at by him. . . hangs down her head when she is asked some question by him, and speaks in indistinct words and unfinished sentences. . . always wears anything that he may have presented to her, becomes dejected when any other bridegroom is mentioned by her parents. . .

love for him; in the case of an elephant woman, the thought that he is a hare man, or a man of weak passion; compassion lest anything should befall him on account of his passion; despair at her own imperfection; fear of discovery; disillusion at seeing his grey hair or shabby appearance; fear that he may be employed by her husband to test her chastity; the thought that he has too much regard for morality.

Whichever of the above causes a man may detect, he should endeavour to remove it from the very beginning. Thus, the bashfulness that may arise from his greatness or his ability, he should remove by showing his great love and affection for her. The difficulty of the want of opportunity, or of his inaccessibility, he should remove by showing her some easy way of access. The excessive respect entertained by the woman for him should be removed by making himself very familiar. The difficulties that arise from his being thought a low character, he should remove by showing his valour and his wisdom; those that come from neglect, by extra attention; and those that arise from fear, by giving her proper encouragement.

The following are the men who generally obtain success with women: men well versed in the science of love; men skilled in telling stories; men acquainted with women from their childhood; men who have secured their confidence; men who send presents to them; men who talk well; men who do things that they like; men who have not loved other women previously; men who act as messengers; men who know their weak points; men who are desired by good women; men who are united with their female friends; men who are good looking; men who have been brought up with them; men who are their neighbours; men who are devoted to sexual pleasures, even though these be their own servants; the lovers of the daughters of their nurse; men who have been lately married; men who like picnics and pleasure parties; men who are liberal; men who are celebrated for being very strong (bull men); enterprising and brave men; men who surpass their husbands in learning and good looks, in good quali-

ties, and in liberality; men whose dress and manner of living are magnificent.

The following are the women who are easily gained over: women who stand at the doors of their houses; women who are always looking out on the street; women who sit conversing in their neighbour's house; a woman who always stares at men; a female messenger; a woman who looks sideways at men; a woman whose husband has taken another wife without any just cause; a woman who hates her husband, or who has not had any children; a woman whose family or caste is not well known; a woman whose children are dead; a woman who is very fond of society; a woman who is apparently very affectionate with her husband; the wife of an actor; a widow; a poor woman; a woman fond of enjoyment; the wife of a man with many younger brothers; a vain woman; a woman whose husband is inferior to her in rank or abilities; a woman who is proud of her skill in the arts; a woman disturbed in mind by the folly of her husband; a woman who has been married in her infancy to a rich man, and not liking him when she grows up, desires a man possessing a disposition, talents, and wisdom suitable to her own tastes; a woman who is slighted by her husband without any cause; a woman who is not respected by other women of the same rank or beauty as herself; a woman whose husband is devoted to travelling; the wife of a jeweller; a jealous woman; a covetous woman; an immoral woman; a barren woman; a lazy woman; a cowardly woman; a humpbacked woman; a dwarfish woman; a deformed woman; a vulgar woman; an ill-smelling woman; a sick woman; an old woman.

There are also two verses on the subject as follows: 'Desire which springs from nature, and which is increased by art, and from which all danger is taken away by wisdom, becomes firm and secure. A clever man, depending on his own ability, and observing carefully the ideas and thoughts of women, and removing the causes of their turning away from men, is generally successful with them.'

II

Of the kinds of women resorted to by the citizens

When *Kama* is practised by men of the four castes according to the rules of the Holy Writ (i.e. by lawful marriage) with virgins of their own caste, it then becomes a means of acquiring lawful progeny and good fame, and it is not also opposed to the customs of the world. On the contrary, the practice of *Kama* with women of the higher castes, and with those previously enjoyed by others, even though they be of the same caste, is prohibited. But the practice of *Kama* with women of the lower castes, with women excommunicated from their own caste, with public women, and with women twice married, is neither enjoined nor prohibited. The object of practising *Kama* with such women is pleasure only. Nayikas, therefore, are of three kinds, viz. maids, women twice married, and public women. Gonikaputra has expressed an opinion that there is a fourth kind of Nayika, viz. a woman who is resorted to on some special occasions even though she be previously married to another. These special occasions are when a man thinks thus:

a) This woman is self-willed, and has been previously enjoyed by many others beside myself. I may, therefore, safely resort to her as a public woman though she belongs to a higher caste than mine, and in so doing, I shall not be violating the ordinances of Dharma.

b) This is a twice-married woman and has been enjoyed by others before me; there is, therefore, no objection to my resorting to her.

c) This woman has gained the heart of her great and powerful husband, and exercises a mastery over him, who is a friend of my enemy; if, therefore, she becomes united with me she will cause her husband to abandon my enemy.

d) This woman will turn the mind of her husband, who is very powerful, in my favour, he being at present disaffected towards me, and intent on doing me some harm.

e) By making this woman my friend I shall gain the object of some friend of mine, or shall be able to effect the ruin of some enemy, or shall accomplish some other difficult purpose.

f) By being united with this woman, I shall kill her husband, and so obtain his vast riches which I covet.

g) The union of this woman with me is not attended with any danger, and will bring me wealth, of which, on account of my poverty and inability to support myself, I am very much in need. I shall, therefore, obtain her vast riches in this way without any difficulty.

h) This woman loves me ardently, and knows all my weak points; if, therefore, I am unwilling to be united with her, she will make my faults public and thus tarnish my character and reputation. Or

she will bring some gross accusation against me, of which it may be hard to clear myself, and I shall be ruined. Or perhaps she will detach from me her husband who is powerful, and yet under her control, and will unite him to my enemy, or will herself join the latter.

i) The husband of this woman has violated the chastity of my wives; I shall therefore return that injury by seducing his wives.

j) By the help of this woman I shall kill an enemy of the king, who has taken shelter with her, and whom I am ordered by the king to destroy.

k) The woman whom I love is under the control of this woman. I shall, through the influence of the latter, be able to get at the former.

l) This woman will bring to me a maid who possesses wealth and beauty, but who is hard to get at, and under the control of another.

m) My enemy is a friend of this woman's husband; I shall therefore cause her to join him, and will thus create an enmity between her husband and him.

For these and similar other reasons the wives of other men may be resorted to, but it must be distinctly understood that is only allowed for special reasons, and not for mere carnal desire.

The following women are not to be enjoyed: a leper; a lunatic; a woman turned out of caste; a woman who reveals secrets; a woman who publicly expresses desire for sexual intercourse; a woman who is extremely white; a woman who is extremely black; a bad-smelling woman; a woman who is a near relation; a woman who is a female friend; a woman who leads the life of an ascetic; and lastly, the wife of a relation, of a friend, of a learned Brahman, and of the king.

The followers of Babhravya say that any woman who has been enjoyed by five men is a fit and proper person to be enjoyed. But Gonikaputra is of the opinion that even when this is the case, the wives of a relation, of a learned Brahman and of a king should be excepted.

The following are of the kind of friends: one who has played with you in the dust, i.e. in childhood; one who is bound by an obligation; one who is of the same disposition and fond of the same things; one who is a fellow student; one who is acquainted with your secrets and faults, and whose faults and secrets are also known to you; one who is a child of your nurse; one who is brought up with you; one who is an hereditary friend.

These friends should possess the following

Above: In the pleasure room, decorated with flowers, and fragrant with perfumes. . . .they may talk suggestively of things which would be considered as coarse, or not to be mentioned generally in society.

Facing page: When a man is endeavouring to seduce one woman, he should not attempt to seduce any other at the same time. But after he has succeeded with the first, and enjoyed her for a considerable time, he can keep her affections by giving her presents that she likes, and then commence making up to another woman.

qualities: they should tell the truth; they should not be changed by time; they should be firm; they should be free from covetousness; they should not be capable of being gained over by others; they should not reveal your secrets.

III

Of examining the state of a woman's mind

When a man is trying to gain over a woman, he should examine the state of her mind, and act as follows. If she listens to him, but does not manifest to him in any way her own intentions, he should then try to gain her over by means of a go-between. If she meets him once, and again comes to meet him better dressed than before, or comes to him in some lonely place, he should be certain that she is capable of being enjoyed by the use of a little force. A woman who lets a man make up to her, but does not give herself up, even after a long time, should be considered as a trifler in love, but owing to the fickleness of the human mind, even such a woman can be conquered by always keeping up a close acquaintance with her.

When a woman avoids the attentions of a man, and on account of respect for him, and pride in herself, will not meet him or approach him, she can be gained over with difficulty, either by endeavouring to keep on familiar terms with her, or else by an exceedingly clever go-between. When a man makes up to a woman, and she reproaches him with harsh words, she should be conquered by patience, and by continued efforts as follows:

If she happens to go to sleep in his vicinity, he should put his left arm round her, and see when she awakes whether she repulses him in reality, or only repulses him in such a way as if she was desirous of the same thing being done to her again. And what is done by the arm can also be done by the foot. If the man succeeds in this point he should embrace her more closely, and if she will not stand the embrace and gets up, but behaves with him as usual the next day, he should consider then that she is not unwilling to be enjoyed by him. If, however, she does not appear again, the man should try to win her over by means of a go-between; and if, after having disappeared for some time, she again appears, and behaves with him as usual, the man should then consider that she would not object to be united with him. When a woman gives a man an opportunity, and makes her own love manifest to him, he should proceed to enjoy her.

When a woman neither gives encouragement to a man, nor avoids him, but hides herself and remains in some lonely place, she must be got at by means of the female servant who may be near her. If, when called by the man, she acts in the same way, then she should be gained over by means of a skilful go-between. But if she will have nothing to say to the man, he should consider well about her before he begins any further attempts to gain her over.

Thus ends the examination of the state of the woman's mind.

A man should first get himself introduced to a woman, and then carry on a conversation with her. He should give her hints of his love for her, and if he finds from her replies that she receives these hints favourably, he should then set to work to gain her over without any fear. A woman who shows her love by outward signs to the man at his first interview, should be gained over very easily. In the same way a lascivious woman, who when addressed in loving words replies openly in words expressive of her love, should be considered to have been gained over at that very moment. With regard to all women, whether they be wise, simple, or confiding, this rule is laid down, that those who make an open manifestation of their love are easily gained over.

Now a girl always shows her love by outward signs and actions, such as the following: she never looks the man in the face, and becomes abashed when she is looked at by him; she looks secretly at him though he has gone away from her side; hangs down her head when she is asked some question by him, and answers in indistinct words and unfinished sentences; delights to be in his company for a long time; speaks to her attendants in a peculiar tone with the hope of attracting his attention towards her when she is at a distance from him; under some pretext or other, makes him look at different things, narrates to him tales and stories very slowly so that she may continue conversing with him for a long time; kisses and embraces before him, a child sitting in her lap; draws ornamental marks on the foreheads of her female servants; performs sportive and graceful movements when her attendants speak jestingly to her in the presence of her lover; confides in her lover's friends, and respects and obeys them; shows kindness to his servants, converses with them, and engages them to do her work as if she were their mistress, and listens attentively to them when they tell stories about her lover to somebody else; enters his house when induced to do so by the daughter of her nurse, and by her assistance manages to converse and play with him; avoids being seen by her lover when she is not dressed and decorated, gives him by the hand of her female friend, her ear ornament, ring, or garland of flowers that he may have asked to see; always wears anything that he may have presented to her, becomes dejected when any other bridegroom is mentioned by her parents, and does not mix with those who may be of his party, or who may support his claims.

There are also some verses on the subject as follows: 'A man who has seen and perceived the feelings of the girl towards him, and who has noticed the outward signs and movements by which those feelings are expressed, should do everything in his power to effect a union with her. He should gain over a young girl by childlike sports, a damsel come-of-age by his skill in the arts, and a girl that loves him by having recourse to persons in whom she confides'.

IV

Of winning over the woman

Ancient authors are of the opinion that girls are not so easily seduced by employing female messengers as by the efforts of the man himself, but that the wives of others are more easily got at by the aid of female messengers than by the personal efforts of the man. But Vatsyayana lays it down that whenever it is possible, a man should always act himself in these matters, and it is only when such is impracticable, or impossible, that female messengers should be employed. As for the saying that women who act and talk boldly and freely are to be won by the personal efforts of the man, and that women who do not possess those qualities are to be got at by female messengers, it is only a matter of talk.

Now when a man acts himself in the matter, he should first of all make the acquaintance of the woman he loves in the following manner:

First, he should arrange to be seen by the woman either on a natural or special opportunity. A natural opportunity is when they meet either at the house of a friend, or a caste-fellow, or a minister or a physician, as also on the occasion of marriage ceremonies, sacrifices, festivals, funerals, and garden parties.

Second, when they do meet, the man should be careful to look at her in such a way as to cause the state of his mind to be made known to her; he should pull about his moustache, make a sound with his nails, cause his own ornaments to tinkle, bite his lower lip, and make various other signs of that description. When she is looking at him, he should speak to his friends and other women about her and should show to her his liberality and his appreciation of enjoyments. When sitting by the side of a female friend, he should yawn and twist his body, contract his eyebrows, speak very slowly as if he was weary, and listen to her indifferently. A conversation having two meanings should also be carried on with a child or some other person, apparently having regard to a third person, but really having reference to the woman he loves, and in this way his love should be made manifest under the pretext of referring to others rather than to herself. He should make marks that have reference to her, on the earth with his nails, or with a stick, and should embrace and kiss a child in her presence, and give it the mixture of betel nut and betel leaves with his tongue, and press its chin with his fingers in a caressing way. All these things should be done at the proper time and in proper places.

Third, the man should fondle a child that may be sitting on her lap, and give it something to play with, and also take the same back again. Conversation with respect to the child may also be held with her, and in this manner he should gradually become well acquainted with her, and he should also make himself agreeable to her relations. Afterwards, this acquaintance should be made a pretext

Above: He should sprinkle upon her the water brought for rinsing his mouth; and when alone with her in a lonely place, or in darkness, he should make love to her, and tell her the true state of his mind. . . though a man loves a girl ever so much, he never succeeds in winning her without a great deal of talking.

Facing page: The congress that takes place between two persons who are attached to one another, and which is done according to their own liking is called 'spontaneous congress'.

for visiting her house frequently, and on such occasions he should converse on the subject of love in her absence, but within her hearing. As his intimacy with her increases he should place in her charge some kind of deposit or trust, and take away from it a small portion at a time; or he may give her some fragrant substances, or betel nuts to be kept for him by her. After this he should endeavour to make her well acquainted with his own wife, and get them to carry on confidential conversations, and to sit together in lonely places. In order to see her frequently, he should arrange so that the same goldsmith, the same jeweller, the same basket maker, the same dyer, and the same washerman should be employed by the two families. And he should also pay her long visits openly under the pretence of being engaged with her on business, and one business should lead to another, so as to keep up the intercourse between them. Whenever she wants anything, or is in need of money, or wishes to acquire skill in one of the arts, he should cause her to understand that he is willing and able to do anything that she wants, to give her money, or teach her one of the arts, all these things being quite within his ability and power. In the same way, he should hold discussions with her in company with other people, and they should talk of the doings and sayings of other persons, and examine different things, like jewellery, precious stones, etc. On such occasions he should show her certain things with the values of which she may be acquainted, and if she begins to dispute with him about the things or their value, he should not contradict her, but point out that he agrees with her in every way.

Thus ends the ways of making the acquaintance of the woman desired.

Now after a girl has become acquainted with the man as above described, and has manifested her love to him by the various outward signs, and by the motions of her body, the man should make every effort to gain her over. But as girls are not acquainted with sexual union, they should be treated with the greatest delicacy, and the man should proceed with considered caution, though in the case of other women, accustomed to sexual intercourse, this is not necessary. When the intentions of the girl are known, and her bashfulness put aside, the man should begin to make use of his money, and an interchange of clothes, rings, and flowers should be made. In this, the man should take particular care that the things given by him are handsome and valuable. He should moreover, receive from her a mixture of betel nut and betel leaves, and when he is going to a party, he should ask for the flower in her hair or for the flower in her hand. If he himself gives her a flower, it should be a sweet smelling one, and marked with marks made by his nails or teeth. With increasing assiduity he should dispel her fears, and by degrees get her to go with him to some lonely place, and there he should embrace and kiss her. And finally at the time of giving her some betel nut, or of receiving the same from her, or at the time of making an exchange of flowers, he should touch and press her private parts, thus bringing his efforts to a satisfactory conclusion.

When a man is endeavouring to seduce one woman, he should not attempt to seduce any other at the same time. But after he has succeeded with the first, and enjoyed her for a considerable time, he can keep her affections by giving her presents that she likes, and then commence making up to another woman. When a man sees the husband of a woman going to some place near his house, he should not enjoy the woman then, even though she may be easily gained over at that time. A wise man, having a regard for his reputation, should not think of seducing a woman who is apprehensive, timid, not to be trusted, well guarded, or possessed of a father-in-law or mother-in-law.

V

Of the art of enticement

If a girl begins to show her love by outward signs and motions, the lover should try to gain her over entirely by various ways and means, such as the following: When engaged with her in any game or sport, he should intentionally hold her hand. He should practise upon her the various kinds of embraces, such as the touching embrace, and others already described in a preceding chapter. He should show her a pair of human beings cut out of the leaf of a tree, and such like things, at intervals. When engaged in water sports, he should dive at a distance from her, and come up close to her. He should show an increased liking for the new foliage of trees and such like things. He should describe to her the pangs he suffers on her account. He should relate to her the beautiful dream that he has had with reference to other women. At parties and assemblies of his caste he should sit near her, and touch her under some pretence or other, and having placed his foot upon hers, he should slowly touch each of her toes, and press the ends of the nails; if successful in this, he should get hold of her foot with his hand and repeat the same thing. He should also press a finger of her hand between his toes, when she happens to be washing his feet; and whenever he gives anything to her or takes anything from her, he should show her by his manner and look how much he loves her.

He should sprinkle upon her the water brought for rinsing his mouth; and when alone with her in a lonely place, or in darkness, he should make love to her, and tell her the true state of his mind without distressing her in any way.

Whenever he sits with her on the same seat or bed, he should say to her, 'I have something to tell you in private,' and then, when she comes to hear it in a quiet place, he should express his love to her more by manner and signs than by words. When he comes to know the state of her feelings towards him he should pretend to be ill, and should make her come to his house to speak to him. There he should intentionally hold her hand, place it on his eyes and forehead, and under the pretence of preparing some medicine for him, he should ask her to do the work for his sake in the following words: 'This work must be done by you, and by nobody else.' When she wants to go away he should let her go, with an earnest request to come and see him again. This device of illness should be continued for three days and three nights. After this, when she begins coming to see him frequently, he should carry on long conversations with her, for, says Chotakamukha, 'Though a man loves a girl ever so much, he never succeeds in winning her without a great deal of talking.' At last when the man finds the girl completely gained over, he may then begin to enjoy her. As for the saying that women grow less timid than usual during the evening, and in darkness, and are desirous of congress at those times, and do not oppose men then, and should only be enjoyed at these hours, it is a matter of talk only.

When it is impossible for the man to carry on his endeavours alone, he should, by means of the daughter of her nurse, or of a female friend in whom she confides, cause the girl to be brought to him without making known to her his design, and he should then proceed with her in the manner above described. Or he should in the beginning, send his own female servant to live with the girl as her friend, and should then gain her over by other means.

At last, when he knows the state of her feelings by her outward manner and conduct towards him at religious ceremonies, marriage ceremonies, fairs, festivals, theatres, public assemblies, and such like occasions, he should begin to enjoy her when she is alone, for Vatsyayana lays it down that women, when resorted to at proper times and in proper places, do not turn away from their lovers.

When a girl, possessed of good qualities and well-bred, though born in a humble family, or destitute of wealth and not therefore desired by her equals, or an orphan girl, or one deprived of her parents, but observing the rules of her family and caste, should wish to bring about her own marriage when she comes of age, such a girl should endeavour to gain over a strong and good looking young man, or a person whom she thinks would marry her on account of the weakness of his mind, and even without the consent of his parents. She should do this by such means as would endear her to the said person, as well as by frequently seeing and meeting him. Her mother also, should constantly cause them to meet by means of her female friends, and the daughter of her nurse. The girl herself should try to get alone with her beloved in some quiet place, and at odd times should give him flowers, betel nut, betel leaves and perfumes. She should also show her skill in the practice of the arts, in shampooing, in scratching and in pressing with the nails. She should also talk to him on the subjects he likes best, and discuss with him the ways and means of gaining over and winning the affections of a girl.

But old authors say that although the girl loves the man ever so much, she should not offer herself, make the first overtures, for a girl who does this loses her dignity, and is liable to be scorned and rejected. But when the man shows his wish to enjoy her, she should be favourable to him and should show no change in her demeanour when he embraces her, and should receive all the mani-

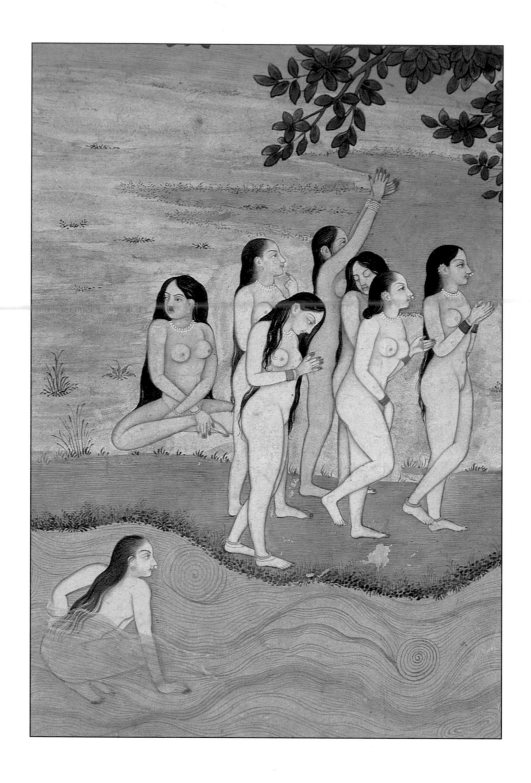

Above: . . . the males simply remove their desire, while the females, from their consciousness of desire, feel a certain kind of pleasure, which gives them satisfaction, but it is impossible for them to tell you what kind of pleasure they feel.

Above: A clever man, learning from the *Shastras* the ways of winning over the wives of other people, is never deceived in the case of his own wives. No one, however, should make use of these ways for seducing the wives of others. . .

festations of his love as if she were ignorant of the state of his mind. But when he tries to kiss her she should oppose him; when he begs to be allowed to have sexual intercourse with her, she should let him touch her private parts only, and with considerable difficulty; and though importuned by him, she should not yield herself up to him as if of her own accord, but should resist his attempts to have her. It is only, moreover, when she is certain that she is truly loved, and that her lover is indeed devoted to her, and will not change his mind, that she should then give herself up to him, and persuade him to marry her quickly. After losing her virginity, she should tell her confidential friends about it.

There are also some verses on the subject as follows: 'A girl who is much sought after should marry the man that she likes, and whom she thinks would be obedient to her, and capable of giving her pleasure. But when from the desire of wealth, a girl is married by her parents to a rich man, without taking into consideration the character or looks of the bridegroom, or when given to a man who has several wives, she never becomes attached to the man, even though he be endowed with good qualities, obedient to her will, active, strong and healthy, and anxious to please her in every way. A husband who is obedient but yet master of himself, though he be poor and not good looking, is better than one who is common to many women, even though he be handsome and attractive. The wives of rich men, where there are many wives, are not generally attached to their husbands, and are not confidential with them, and even though they possess all the external enjoyments of life, still have recourse to other men. A man who is of a low mind, who has fallen from his social position, and who is much given to travelling, does not deserve to be married; neither does one who has many wives and children, or one who is devoted to sport and gambling, and who comes to his wife only when he likes. Of all the lovers of a girl, he only is her true husband who possesses the qualities that are liked by her, and such a husband only enjoys real superiority over her, because he is the husband of love.'

VI

Of other forms of marriage

When a girl cannot meet her lover frequently in private, she should send the daughter of her nurse to him, it being understood that she has confidence in her, and had previously gained her over to her interests. On seeing the man, the daughter of the nurse should, in the course of conversation, describe to him the noble birth, the good disposition, the beauty, talent, skill, knowledge of human nature and affection of the girl in such a way as not to let him suppose that she had been sent by the girl, and should thus create affection for the girl in the heart of the man. To the girl also, she should speak about the excellent qualities of the man, especially of those qualities which she knows are pleasing to the girl. When the girl is gained over, and acts openly with the man as his wife, he should cause fire to be brought from the house of a Brahman, and having spread the Kusha grass upon the ground, and offered an oblation to the fire, he should marry her according to the precepts of the religious law. After this, he should inform his parents of the fact, because it is the opinion of ancient authors that a marriage solemnly contracted in the presence of fire cannot afterwards be set aside.

After the consummation of the marriage, the relations of the man should gradually be made acquainted with the affair, and the relations of the girl should also be apprised of it in such a way, that they may consent to the marriage, and overlook the manner in which it was brought about, and when this is done, they should afterwards be reconciled by affectionate presents and favourable conduct. In this manner the man should marry the girl according to the Gandharva form of marriage.

When the girl cannot make up her mind, or will not express her readiness to marry, the man should obtain her in any one of the following ways:

1) On a fitting occasion, and under some excuse, he should, by means of a female friend with whom he is well acquainted and whom he can trust, and who also is well known to the girl's family, get the girl brought unexpectedly to his house, and he should then bring fire from the house of a Brahman, and proceed as before described.

2) When the marriage of the girl with some other person draws near, the man should disparage the future husband to the utmost in the mind of the mother of the girl, and then having got the girl to come with her mother's consent, to a neighbouring house, he should bring fire from the house of a Brahman, and proceed as above.

3) The man should become a great friend of the brother of the girl, the said brother being of the same age as himself, and addicted to courtesans, and to intrigues with the wives of other people, and should give him assistance in such matters, and also give him occasional presents. He should then tell him about his great love for his sister, as young men will sacrifice even their lives for the sake of those who may be of the same age, habits, and disposition as themselves. After this, the man should get the girl brought by means of her brother, to some secure place, and having brought fire from the house of a Brahman should proceed as before.

4) The man should on the occasion of festivals, get the daughter of the nurse to give the girl some intoxicating substance, and then cause her to be brought to some secure place under the pretence of some business, and there having enjoyed her before she recovers from her intoxication, should bring fire from the house of a Brahman, and proceed as before.

5) The man should, with the connivance of the daughter of the nurse, carry off the girl from her house while she is asleep, and then, having enjoyed her before she recovers from her sleep, should bring fire from the house of a Brahman, and proceed as before.

There are verses on this subject as follows. 'In all the forms of marriage given in this chapter of this work, the one that precedes is better than the one that follows it, on account of it being more in accordance with the commands of religion, and therefore it is only when it is impossible to carry the former into practice, that the latter should be resorted to. As the fruit of all good marriages is love, the Gandharva form of marriage is respected, even though it is formed under unfavourable circumstances, because it fulfils the object sought for. Another cause of respect accorded to this form of marriage is, that it brings forth happiness, causes less trouble in its performance than the other forms of marriage and is above all, the result of previous love.

VII

Of the women of the royal harem, and the keeping of one's own wife

The women of the royal harem cannot see or meet any men on account of their being strictly guarded, neither do they have their desires satisfied, because their only husband is common to many wives. For this reason, among themselves, they give pleasure to each other in various ways as now described. Having dressed the daughters of their nurses, or their female friends, or their female attendants, like men, they accomplish their object by means of bulbs, roots, and fruits having the form of the *lingam*, or they lie down upon the statue of a male figure, in which the *lingam* is visible and erect.

Some kings, who are compassionate, take or apply certain medicines, to enable them to enjoy many wives in one night, simply for the purpose of satisfying the desire of their women, though they perhaps have no desire of their own. Others enjoy with great affection only those wives that they particularly like, while others only take them, according as the turn of each wife arrives in due course. Such are the ways of enjoyment prevalent in Eastern countries, and what is said about the means of enjoyment of the female, is also applicable to the male. By means of their female attendants, the ladies of the royal harem generally get men into their apartments in the disguise or dress of women. Their female attendants, and the daughters of their nurses, who are acquainted with their secrets, should exert themselves to get men to come to the harem in this way, by telling them of the good fortune attending it, and by describing the facilities of entering and leaving the palace, the large size of the premises, the carelessness of the sentinels, and the irregularities of the attendants about the persons of the royal wives. But these women should never induce a man to enter the harem by telling him falsehoods, for that would probably lead to his destruction.

As for the man himself, he had better not enter a royal harem, even though it may be easily accessible, on account of the numerous disasters to

Above: The women of the royal harem cannot see or meet any men on account of their being strictly guarded, neither do they have their desires satisfied, because their only husband is common to many wives. For this reason, among themselves, they give pleasure to each other in various ways. . .

Facing page: . . . when engaged with her in any game or sport, he should intentionally hold her hand. He should practise upon her the various kinds of embraces, such as the touching embrace. . . he should describe to her the pangs he suffers on her account.

which he may be exposed there. If however, he wants to enter it, he should first ascertain whether there is an easy way to get out, whether it is closely surrounded by the pleasure garden, whether it has separate enclosures belonging to it, whether the sentinels are careless, whether the king has gone abroad, and then, when he is called by the women of the harem, he should carefully observe the localities, and enter by the way pointed out by them. If he is able to manage it, he should hang about the harem every day, and under some pretext or other, make friends with the sentinels, and show himself attached to the female attendants of the harem, who may have become acquainted with his design, and to whom he should express his regret at not being able to obtain the object of his desire. Lastly, he should cause the whole business of a go-between to be done by the women who may have access to the harem, and he should be careful to be able to recognize the emissaries of the king.

When a go-between has no access to the harem, then the man should stand in some place where the lady whom he loves, and whom he is anxious to enjoy, can be seen. If that place is occupied by the king's sentinels, he should then disguise himself as a female attendant of the lady who comes to the place, or passes by it. When she looks at him, he should let her know his feelings by outward signs and gestures, and should show her pictures, things with double meanings, chaplets of flowers, and rings. He should carefully mark the answer she gives, whether by word or sign, or by gesture, and should then try and get into the harem. If he is certain of her coming to some particular place, he should conceal himself there, and at the appointed time should enter along with her, as one of the guards.

The entrance of young men into harems, and their exit from them, generally take place when things are being brought into the palace, or when things are being taken out of it, or when drinking festivals are going on, or when the female attendants are in a hurry, or when the residence of some of the royal ladies is being changed, or when the king's wives go to gardens, or to fairs, or when they enter the palace on their return from them, or lastly, when the king is absent on a long pilgrimage. The women of the royal harem know each other's secrets, and having but one object to attain, they give assistance to each other. A young man, who enjoys all of them, and who is common to them all, can continue enjoying his union with them so long as it is kept quiet, and is not known abroad.

For these reasons, a man should guard his own wife. Old authors say that a king should select for sentinels in his harem, such men as have their freedom from carnal desires well tested. But such men, though free themselves from carnal desire, by reason of their fear or avarice, may cause other persons to enter the harem, and therefore Gonikaputra says, that kings should place such men in the harem as may have had their freedom from carnal desires, their fears, and their avarice well tested. Lastly Vatsyayana says, that under the influence of *Dharma* people might be admitted, and therefore, men should be selected who are free from carnal desires, fear, avarice, and *Dharma*.

The followers of Babhravya say, that a man should cause his wife to associate with a young woman who would tell him the secrets of other people, and thus find out from her, about his wife's chastity. But Vatsyayana says, a man should not cause his innocent wife to be corrupted by bringing her into the company of a deceitful woman.

The following are the causes of the destruction of a woman's chastity: always going into society, and sitting in company; absence of restraint; the loose habits of her husband; want of caution in her relations with other men; continued and long absence of her husband; living in a foreign country; destruction of her love and feelings by her husband; the company of loose women; the jealousy of her husband.

There are also the following verses on the subject: 'A clever man, learning from the Shastras the ways of winning over the wives of other people, is never deceived in the case of his own wives. No one, however, should make use of these ways for seducing the wives of others, because they do not always succeed, and moreover, often cause disasters, and the destruction of *Dharma* and *Artha*. This book, which is intended for the good of the people, and to teach them the ways of guarding their own wives, should not be made use of merely for gaining over the wives of others.'

PART

On Marriage

I

Of acquiring the right kind of wife

When a girl of the same caste and a virgin is married in accordance with the precepts of the Holy Writ, the results of such a union are: the acquisition of *Dharma* and *Artha*, offspring, affinity, increase of friends, and untarnished love. For this reason a man should fix his affection upon a girl who is of good family, whose parents are alive, and who is three years or more younger than himself. She should be born of a highly respectable family, possessed of wealth, well connected, and with many relations and friends. She should also be beautiful, of a good disposition, with lucky marks on her body, and with good hair, nails, teeth, ears, eyes, and breasts neither more nor less than they ought to be, and no one of them entirely wanting, and not troubled with a sickly body. The man should, of course, also possess these qualities himself. But at all events, says Ghotakamukha, a girl who has been already joined with others (i.e. no longer a maiden) should never be loved, for it would be reproachable to do such a thing. Now in order to bring about a marriage with such a girl as described above, the parents and relations of the man should exert themselves, as also such friends on both sides as may desire to assist in the matter.

These friends should bring to the notice of the girl's parents the faults, both present and future, of all the other men that may wish to marry her, and should at the same time extol, even to exaggeration, all the excellences, ancestral and paternal, of their friend, so as to endear him to them, and particularly to those that may be liked by the girl's mother. One of the friends should also disguise himself as an astrologer, and declare the future good fortune and wealth of his friend by showing the existence of all the lucky omens and signs, the good influence of planets, the auspicious entrance of the sun into a sign of the Zodiac, propitious stars and fortunate marks on his body. Others again should rouse the jealousy of the girl's mother by telling her that their friend has a chance of getting from some other quarter, even a better girl than hers.

A girl should be taken as a wife or given in marriage, when fortune, signs, omens, and the words of others are favourable, for, says Ghotakamukha, a man should not marry at any time he likes. A girl who is asleep, crying, or gone out of the house when sought in marriage, or who is betrothed to another, should not be married. The following also should be avoided: one who is kept concealed; one who has an ill-

Above: A man marrying many wives should act fairly towards them all. He should neither disregard nor pass over their faults, and should not reveal to one wife the love, passion, bodily blemishes, and confidential reproaches of another. . . he should please them all by going to gardens, by amusements, by presents, by honouring their relations, by telling them secrets, and lastly by loving unions.

Facing page: Love which is felt for things to which we are not habituated, and which proceeds entirely from ideas, is called love resulting from imagination.

sounding name; one who has her nose depressed; one who has her nostril turned up; one who is formed like a male; one who is bent down; one who has crooked thighs; one who has a projecting forehead; one who has a bald head; one who does not like purity; one who has been polluted by another; one who is affected with the *gulma*; one who is disfigured in any way; one who has not fully arrived at puberty; one who is a friend; one who is a younger sister; one who is a Varshakari.

In the same way, a girl who is called by the name of one of the twenty-seven stars, or by the name of a tree, or of a river, is considered worthless, as also a girl whose name ends in 'r' or 'l'. But some authors say that prosperity is gained only by marrying the girl to whom one becomes attached, and that therefore, no other girl but the one who is loved should be married by anyone.

When a girl becomes marriageable, her parents should dress her smartly, and should place her where she can be easily seen by all. Every afternoon, having dressed her and decorated her in a becoming manner, they should send her with her female companions to sports, sacrifices, and marriage ceremonies, and thus show her to advantage in society, because she is a kind of merchandise. They should also receive, with kind words and signs of friendliness, those of an auspicious appearance who may come, accompanied by their friends and relations for the purpose of marrying their daughter, and under some pretext or other having first dressed her becomingly, should then present her to them.

After this they should await the pleasure of fortune, and with this object, should appoint a future day on which a determination could be come to with regard to their daughter's marriage. On this occasion, when the persons have come, the parents of the girl should ask them to bathe and dine, and should say, 'Everything will take place at the proper time,' and should not then comply with the request, but should settle the matter later.

When a girl is thus acquired, either according to the custom of the country, or according to his own desire, the man should marry her in accordance with the precepts of the Holy Writ, according to one of the four kinds of marriage.

Amusement in society, such as completing verses begun by others, marriages, and auspicious ceremonies should be carried on neither with superiors, nor inferiors, but with equals. That should be known as a high connection when a man, after marrying a girl, has to serve her and her relations afterwards like a servant, and such a connection is censured by the good. On the other hand, that reproachable connection, where a man together with his relations, lords it over his wife, is called a low connection by the wise. But when both the man and the woman afford mutual pleasure to each other, and when the relatives on both sides pay respect to one another, such is called a connection in the proper sense of the word. Therefore, a man should contract neither a high connection by which he is obliged to bow down afterwards to his kinsmen, nor a low connection, which is universally reprehended by all.

II

Of creating confidence in the girl

For the first three days after marriage, the girl and her husband should sleep on the floor, abstain from sexual pleasures, and eat their food without seasoning it either with alkali or salt. For the next seven days they should bathe amidst the sounds of auspicious musical instruments, should decorate themselves, dine together and pay attention to their relations as well as to those who may have come to witness their marriage. This is applicable to persons of all castes. On the night of the tenth day, the man

should begin in a lonely place with soft words, and thus create confidence in the girl. Some authors say that for the purpose of winning her over, he should not speak to her for three days, but the followers of Babhravya are of the view that if the man does not speak with her for three days, the girl may be discouraged by seeing him spiritless like a pillar, and becoming dejected, she may begin to despise him as a eunuch. Vatsyayana says that the man should begin to win her over and to create confidence in her, but should abstain at first from sexual pleasures. Women being of a tender nature, want tender beginnings, and when they are forcibly approached by men with whom they are but slightly acquainted, they sometimes suddenly become haters of sexual connection, and sometimes even haters of the male sex.

The man should therefore approach the girl according to her liking, and should make use of those devices by which he may be able to establish himself more and more into her confidence.

When the girl accepts the embrace, the man should put a 'tambula' or screw of betel nut and betel leaves in her mouth, and if she will not take it, he should induce her to do so by conciliatory words, entreaties, oaths, and kneeling at her feet, for it is a universal rule, that however bashful or angry a woman may be, she never disregards a man kneeling at her feet. At the time of giving this 'tambula' he should kiss her mouth softly and gracefully, without making any sound. When she is gained over in this respect he should then make her talk, and so that she may be induced to talk he should ask questions about things of which he knows or pretends to know nothing, and which can be answered in a few words. If she does not speak to him, he should not frighten her, but should ask her the same thing again and again in a conciliatory manner. If she does not then speak he should urge her to give a reply, because as Ghotakamukha says, 'All girls hear everything said to them by men, but do not themselves sometimes say a single word.' When she is thus importuned, the girl should give replies by shakes of the head, but if she is annoyed with the man, she should not even do that. When she is asked by the man whether she wishes for him, and whether she likes him, she should remain silent for a long time, and when at last importuned to reply, should give him a favourable answer by a nod of her head. If the man is previously acquainted with the girl, he should converse with her by means of a female friend, who may be favourable to him, and in the confidence of both, and carry on the conversation on both sides. On such an occasion, the girl should smile with her head bent down, and if the female friend says more on her part than she was desired to do, she should chide her and dispute with her. The female friend should say in jest

even what she is not desired to say by the girl, and add, 'she says so,' on which the girl should say indistinctly and prettily, 'Oh no! I did not say so,' and she should then smile and throw an occasional glance towards the man.

If the girl is familiar with the man, she should place near him without saying anything, the 'tambula', the ointment, or the garland that he may have asked for, or she may tie them up in his upper garment. While she is engaged in this, the man should touch her young breasts in the sounding way of pressing with the nails, and if she prevents him doing this, he should say to her, 'I will not do it again if you will embrace me,' and should in this way cause her to embrace him. While he is being embraced by her, he should pass his hand repeatedly over and about her body. By and by he should place her in his lap, and try more and more to gain her consent, and if she will not yield to him he should frighten her by saying, 'I shall impress marks of my teeth and nails on your lips and breasts, and then make similar marks on my own body and shall tell my friends that you did them. What will you say then?' In this and other ways, as fear and confidence are created in the minds of children, so should the man gain her over to his wishes.

On the second and third nights, after her confidence has increased still more, he should feel the whole of her body with his hand, and kiss her all over; he should also place his hands upon her thighs and shampoo them, and if he succeeds in this, he should then shampoo the joints of her thighs. If she tries to prevent him doing this he should say to her, 'What harm is there in doing it?' and should persuade her to let him do it. After gaining this point he should touch her private parts, should loosen her girdle and the knot of her dress, and turning up her lower garment should shampoo the joints of her naked thighs. Under various pretences he should do all these things, but he should not at that time begin actual congress. After this he should teach her the sixty-four arts, should tell her how much he loves her, and describe to her the hopes which he formerly entertained regarding her. He should also promise to be faithful to her in future, and should dispel all her fears with respect to rival women, and, at last, after having overcome her bashfulness, he should begin to enjoy her in a

Above: When a woman stands on her hands and feet like a quadruped, and her lover mounts her like a bull, it is called the 'congress of a cow'. At this time, everything that is normally done on the bosom should be done on the back. In the same way can be carried on the congress of a dog, the congress of a goat, the congress of a deer. . . and in all these cases the characteristics of these different animals should be manifested by acting like them.

Facing page: When a lover comes to her abode, a courtesan should entertain him with a long conversation. . . and at the same time should show him her skill in sexual enjoyment.

way so as not to frighten her. So much about creating confidence in the girl; and there are, moreover, some verses on the subject as follows:

'A man acting according to the inclinations of a girl, should try and gain her over so that she may love him and place her confidence in him. A man does not succeed either by implicitly following the inclinations of a girl, or by wholly opposing her, and he should, therefore, adopt a middle course. He who knows how to make himself beloved by women, as well as to increase their honour and create confidence in them, this man becomes an object of their love. But he who neglects a girl thinking she is too bashful, is despised by her as a beast ignorant of the workings of the female mind. Moreover, a girl forcibly enjoyed by one who does not understand the hearts of girls becomes nervous, uneasy, and dejected, and suddenly begins to hate the man who has taken advantage of her; and then, when her love is not understood or returned, she sinks into despondency and becomes either a hater of mankind altogether, or, hating her own man, she has recourse to other men.'

III

Of living as a virtuous wife

A virtuous woman, who has affection for her husband, should act in conformity with his wishes as if he were a divine being, and with his consent should take upon herself the whole care of his family. she should keep the whole house well cleaned, and arrange flowers of various kinds in different parts of it, and make the floor smooth and polished so as to give the whole a neat and becoming appearance. She should surround the house with a garden, and place ready in it all the materials required for the morning, noon and evening sacrifices. Moreover, she should herself revere the sanctuary of the household gods, for says Gonardiya, 'Nothing so much attracts the heart of a householder to his wife as a careful observance of the things mentioned above.'

Towards the parents, relations, friends, sisters, and servants of her husband she should behave as they deserve. In the garden she should plant beds of green vegetables, bunches of sugar cane, and clumps of the fig tree, the mustard plant, the parsley plant, the fennel plant, and the *xanthochymus pictorius*. Clusters of various flowers such as the *trapa bispinosa*, the jasmine, the *gasminum grandiflorum*, the yellow amaranth, the wild jasmine, the *tabernamontana coronaria*, the nadyawort, the china rose and others, should likewise be planted, together with the fragrant grass *andropogon schaenanthus*, and the fragrant root of the plant *andropogon miricatus*. She should also have seats and arbours made in the garden, in the middle of which a well, tank, or pool should be dug.

The wife should always avoid the company of female beggars and mendicants, unchaste and roguish women, female fortune tellers and witches. As regards meals she should always consider what her husband likes and dislikes, and what things are good for him and what are injurious to him. When she hears the sounds of his footsteps coming home she should at once get up, and be ready to do whatever he may command her, and either order her female servant to wash his feet, or wash them herself. When going anywhere with her husband, she should put on her ornaments, and without his consent she should not either give or accept invitations, or attend marriages and sacrifices, or sit in the company of female friends, or visit the temples of the gods. And if she wants to engage in any kind of games or sports, she should not do it against his will. In the same way she should always sit down after him, and get up before him, and should never awaken him when he is asleep. The kitchen should be situated in a quiet and retired place, so as not to be accessible to strangers, and should always look clean.

In the event of any misconduct on the part of her husband, she should not blame him excessively, though she be a little displeased. She should not use abusive language towards him, but rebuke him with conciliatory words, whether he be in the company of friends or alone. Moreover, she should not be a scold, for says Gonardiya, 'There is no cause of dislike on the part of a husband so great as this characteristic in a wife.' Lastly, she should avoid bad expressions, sulky looks, speaking aside, standing in the doorway and looking at passers-by, conversing in the pleasure groves, and remaining in a lonely place for a long time; and finally she should always keep her body, her teeth, her hair and everything belonging to her tidy, sweet, and clean.

When the wife wants to approach her husband in private, her dress should consist of many ornaments, various kinds of flowers, and a cloth decorated with different colours, and some sweet-smelling ointments or unguents. But her everyday dress should be composed of a thin close-textured cloth, a few ornaments and flowers, and a little scent, not too much. She should also observe the fasts and vows of her husband, and when he tries to prevent her doing this, she should persuade him to let her do it.

At appropriate times of the year, and when they happen to be cheap, she should buy earth, bamboos, firewood, skins, and iron pots, as also salt and oil. Fragrant substances, vessels made of the fruit of the plant *wrightea antidysenterica*, or oval leaved *wrightea*; medicines, and other things which are always wanted, should be obtained when required and kept in a secret place of the house. The seeds of the radish, the potato, the common beet, the Indian wormwood, the mango, the cucumber, the egg plant, the *kushmanda*, the pumpkin gourd, the *surana*, the *bignonia indica*, the sandalwood, the *premna spinosa*, the garlic plant, the onion, and other vegetables, should be bought and sown at the proper seasons.

The wife, moreover, should not tell to strangers the amount of her wealth, nor the secrets which her husband has confided to her. She should surpass all the women of her own rank in life in her cleverness, her appearance, her knowledge of cookery, her pride, and her manner of serving her husband. The expenditure of the year should be regulated by the profits. The milk that remains after the meals should be turned into ghee or clarified butter. Oil and sugar should be prepared at home; spinning and weaving should also be done there; and a store of ropes and cords, and barks of trees for twisting into ropes should be kept. She should also attend to the pounding and cleaning of rice, using its small grain and chaff in some way or other. She should pay the salaries of the servants, look after tilling of the fields, and take care of the rams, cocks, qulais, parrots, starlings, cuckoos, peacocks, monkeys, and deer; and finally adjust the income and expenditure of the day. The worn-out clothes should be given to those servants who have done good work, in order to show them that their services have been appreciated, or they may be applied to some other use. The vessels in which wine is prepared, as well as those in which it is kept, should be carefully looked after, and put away at the proper time. All sales and purchases should also be well attended to. The friends of her husband she should welcome by presenting them with flowers, ointment, incense, betel leaves, and betel nut. Her father-in-law and mother-in-law she should treat as they deserve, always remaining dependent on their will, never contradicting them, speaking to them in few and not harsh words, not laughing loudly in their presence, and acting with their friends and enemies as with her own. In addition to the above, she should not be vain, or too much taken up with her enjoyments. She should be liberal towards her servants, and reward them on holidays and festivals, and not give away anything without first making it known to her husband.

Thus ends the manner of living of a virtuous woman.

During the absence of her husband on a journey, the virtuous woman should wear only her auspicious ornaments, and observe the fasts in honour of the gods. While anxious to hear the news of her husband, she should still look after her household affairs. She should sleep near the elder women of the house, and make herself agreeable to them. She should look after and keep in repair the things that are liked by her husband, and continue the works that have been begun by him. She should not go to the abode of her relations except on occasions of joy and sorrow, and then she should go in her usual travelling dress, accompanied by her husband's servants, and not remain there for a long time. The fasts and feasts should be observed with the consent of the elders of the house. The resources should be increased by making purchases and sales according to the practice of the merchants, and by means of honest servants, superintended

Above: From the very beginning, a wife should endeavour to attract the heart of her husband by showing to him continually her devotion, her good temper, and her wisdom. If however, she bears him no children, she should herself tell her husband to marry another woman. And when the second wife is married, and brought to the house, the first wife should give her a position superior to her own, and look upon her as a sister.

Above: During the absence of her husband on a journey, the virtuous woman should wear only her auspicious ornaments, and observe the fasts in honour of the gods. And when her husband returns from his journey, she should receive him, at first in her ordinary clothes so that he may know in what way she has lived during his absence, and should bring to him some presents, as also materials for the worship of the deity.

by herself. The income should be increased, and the expenditure diminished as much as possible. And when her husband returns from his journey, she should receive him, at first in her ordinary clothes so that he may know in what way she has lived during his absence, and should bring to him some presents, and also materials for the worship of the deity.

Thus ends the part relating to the behaviour of a wife during the absence of her husband on journey.

There are also some verses on the subject as follows: 'The wife, whether she be a woman of noble family, or a virgin widow remarried, or a concubine, should lead a chaste life, devoted to her husband, and doing everything for his welfare. Women acting thus, acquire *Dharma*, *Artha*, and *Kama*, obtain a high postion, and generally keep their husbands devoted to them.'

IV

Of the conduct of husbands and wives

The causes of re-marrying during the lifetime of the wife are as follows: the folly or ill temper of the wife; her husband's dislike of her; the want of offspring; the continual birth of daughters; the incontinence of the husband.

From the very beginning, a wife should endeavour to attract the heart of her husband by showing to him continually her devotion, her good temper, and her wisdom. If however, she bears him no children, she should herself tell her husband to marry another woman. And when the second wife is married, and brought to the house, the wife should give her a position superior to her own, and look upon her as a sister. In the morning, the elder wife should forcibly make the younger one decorate herself in the presence of their husband, and should not mind all the husband's favour being given to her. If the younger wife does anything to displease her husband, the elder one should not neglect her, but should always be ready to give her most careful advice, and should teach her to do various things in the presence of her husband. Her children she should treat as her own, her attendants she should look upon with more regard even than on her own servants, her friends she should cherish with love and kindness, and her relations with great honour.

When there are many other wives besides herself, the elder wife should associate with the one who is immediately next to her in rank and age, and should instigate the wife who has recently enjoyed her husband's favour to quarrel with the present favourite. After this she should sympathize with the former, and having collected all the other wives together, should get them to denounce the favourite as a scheming and wicked woman, without however committing herself in any way. If the favourite wife happens to quarrel with the husband, then the elder wife should take her part and give her false encouragement, and thus cause the quarrel to be increased. If there be only a little quarrel between the two, the elder wife should do all she can to work it up into a large quarrel. But if after all this, she finds the husband still continues to love his favourite wife, she should then change her tactics, and endeavour to bring about a conciliation between them, so as to avoid her husband's displeasure. Thus ends the conduct of the elder wife.

The younger wife should regard the elder wife of her husband as her mother, and should not give anything away, even to her own relations, without her knowledge. She should tell her everything about herself, and not approach her husband without her permission. Whatever is told to her by the elder wife she should not reveal to others, and she should take care of the children of the senior even more than of her own. When alone with her husband she should serve him well, but should not tell him of the pain she suffers from the existence of a rival wife. She may also obtain secretly from her husband some marks of his particular regard for her, and may tell him that she lives only for him, and for the regard that he has for her. She should never reveal her love for her husband, nor her husband's love for her to any person, either in pride or in anger, for a wife that reveals the secrets of her husband is despised by him. As for seeking to obtain the regard of her husband, Gonardiya says, this should always be done in private, for fear of the elder wife. If the elder wife be disliked by her husband, or be childless, she should sympathize with her, and should ask her husband to do the same, but should surpass her in leading the life of a chaste woman. Thus ends the conduct of the younger wife towards the elder.

A widow in poor circumstances, or of a weak nature, and who allies herself again to a man, is called a widow re-married. The followers of Babhravya say that a virgin widow should not marry a person whom she may be obliged to leave on account of his bad character, or of his being destitute of the excellent qualities of a man, she thus being obliged to have recourse to another person. Gonardiya is of the opinion that as the cause of a widow marrying again is her desire for happiness, and as happiness is secured by the possession of excellent qualities in her husband, joined to love of enjoyment, it is better therefore, to secure a person endowed with such qualities in the first instance. Vatsyayana however, thinks that a widow may marry any person that she likes, and that she thinks will suit her.

At the time of her marriage, the widow should obtain from her husband the money to pay the costs of drinking parties, and picnics with her relations, and of giving them and her friends kindly gifts and presents; or she may do these things at her own cost if she likes. In the same way, she may wear either her husband's ornaments or her own. As to the presents of affection mutually exchanged between the husband and herself, there is no fixed rule about them. If she leaves her husband after marriage of her own accord, she should restore to him whatever he may have given her, with the exception of the mutual presents. If however, she is driven out of the house by her husband, she should not return anything to him.

After her marriage, she should live in the house of her husband like one of the chief members of the family, but should treat the other ladies of the family with kindness, the servants with generosity, and all the friends of the house with familiarity and good temper. She should show that she is better acquainted with the sixty-four arts than the other ladies of the house, and in any quarrels with her husband, she should not rebuke him severely, but in private do everything that he wishes, and make use of the sixty-four ways of enjoyment. She should be obliging to the other wives of her husband, and to their children she should give presents, behave as their mistress, and make ornaments and playthings for their use. In the friends and servants of her husband she should confide more than in his other wives, and finally she should have a liking for drinking parties, going to picnics, attending fairs and festivals, and for carrying out all kinds of games and amusements. Thus ends the conduct of a virgin widow re-married.

A woman who is disliked by her husband, and annoyed and distressd by his other wives, should associate with the wife who is liked most by her husband, and who serves him more than the others, and should teach her all the arts with which she is acquainted. She should act as the nurse of her husband's children, and having gained over his friends to her side, should through them make him acquainted of her devotion to him. In religious ceremonies she should be a leader, as also in vows and fasts, and should not hold too good an opinion of herself. When her husband is lying on his bed, she should only go near him when it is agreeable to him, and should never rebuke him, or show obstinacy in any way. If her husband happens to quarrel with any of his other wives, she should reconcile them to each other, and if he desires to see any woman secretly, she should manage to bring about the meeting between them. She should, moreover, make herself acquainted with the weak points of her husband's character, but always keep them secret, and on the whole behave herself in such a way as may lead him to look upon her as a good and devoted wife. Here ends the conduct of a wife disliked by her husband.

A man marrying many wives should act fairly towards them all. He should neither disregard nor pass over their faults, and should not reveal to one wife the love, passion, bodily blemishes, and confidential reproaches of the other. No opportunity should be given to any one of them of speaking to him about their rivals, and if one of them should begin to speak ill of another, he should chide her and tell her that she has exactly the same blemishes in her character. One of them he should please by secret confidence,

Above: The characteristics of manhood are said to consist of roughness and impetuosity, while weakness, tenderness, sensibility, and an inclination to turn away from unpleasant things are the distinguishing marks of womanhood. The excitement of passion, and peculiarities of habit may sometimes cause contrary results to appear, but these do not last long, and in the end the natural state is resumed.

Facing page: Some kings, who are compassionate, take or apply certain medicines, to enable them to enjoy many wives in one night, simply for the purpose of satisfying the desire of their women, though they perhaps have no desire of their own. Others enjoy with great affection only those wives that they particularly like, while others only take them, according as the turn of each wife arrives in due course.

another by secret respect, and another by secret flattery, and he should please them all by going to gardens, by amusements, by presents, by honouring their relations, by telling them secrets, and lastly by loving unions. A young woman who is of a good temper, and who conducts herself according to the precepts of the Holy Writ, wins her husband's attachment, and obtains a superiority over her rivals.

V

Of manifestation of the feelings by outward signs and deeds

A poor man possessed of good qualities, a man born of a low family possessed of mediocre qualities, a neighbour possessed of wealth, and one under the control of his father, mother or brothers, should not marry without endeavouring to gain over the girl from her childhood, to love and esteem them. Thus a boy separated from his parents, and living in the house of his uncle, should try to gain over the daughter of his uncle, or some other girl, even though she be previously betrothed to another. And this way of gaining over a girl, says Ghotakamukha, is unexpectional, because *Dharma* can be accomplished by means of it, as well as by any other way of marriage.

When a boy has thus begun to woo the girl he loves, he should spend his time with her and amuse her with various games and diversions fitted for their age and acquaintanceship, such as picking and collecting flowers, making garlands of flowers, playing the roles of members of a fictitious family, cooking food, playing with dice, playing with cards, the game of odd and even, the game of finding out the middle finger, the game of six pebbles, and such other games as may be prevalent in the country, and agreeable to the disposition of the girl. In addition to this, he should carry on various amusing games played by several persons together, such as hide and seek, playing with seeds, hiding things in several small heaps of wheat and looking for them, blind-man's buff, gymnastic exercises, and other games of the sort, in company with the girl, her friends and female attendants. The man should also show great kindness to any woman whom the girl thinks fit to be trusted, and should also make new acquaintances, but above all he should attach to himself by kindness and little services, the daughter of the girl's nurse, for if she be gained over, even though she comes to know of his design, she does not cause any obstruction, but is sometimes even able to effect an union between him and the girl. And though she knows the true character of the man, she always talks of his many excellent qualities to the parents and relations of the girl, even though she may not be desired to do so by him.

In the next place he should get her to meet him in some place privately, and should then tell her that the reason of his giving presents to her in secret was the fear that the parents of both of them might be displeased, and then he may add that the things which he had given her had been much desired by other people. When her love begins to show signs of increasing, he should relate to her agreeable stories if she expresses a wish to hear such narratives. Or if she takes delight in legerdemain, he should amaze her by performing various tricks of jugglery; or if she feels a great curiosity to see a performance of the various arts, he should show his own skill in them. When she is delighted with singing he should entertain her with music, and festivals, and at the time of her return after being absent from home, he should present her with bouquets of flowers, and with chaplets for the head, and with ear ornaments and rings, for these are the proper occasions on which such things should be presented.

He should also teach the daughter of the girl's nurse all the sixty-four means of pleasure practised by men, and under this pretext should also inform her of his great skill in the art of sexual enjoyment. All this time he should wear a fine dress, and make as good an appearance as possible, for young women love men who live with them, and who are handsome, good looking and well dressed. As for the saying that though women may fall in love, they still make no effort themselves to gain over the object of their affections, that is only a matter of idle talk.

Part

IV

On Courtesans

I

Of the causes of a courtesan resorting to men, and of the means of attaching to herself the man desired

By having intercourse with men courtesans obtain sexual pleasure, as well as their own maintenance. Now when a courtesan takes up with a man from love, the action is natural; but when she resorts to him for the purpose of getting money, her action is artificial or forced. Even in the latter case, however, she should conduct herself as if her love were indeed natural, because men repose their confidence in those women who apparently love them. In making known her love to the man, she should show an entire freedom from avarice, and for the sake of her future credit, she should abstain from acquiring money from him by unlawful means.

A courtesan, well dressed and wearing her ornaments, should sit or stand at the door of her house, and without exposing herself too much, should look on the public road so as to be seen by the passers-by, she being like an object on view for sale. She should form friendships with such persons as would enable her to separate men from other women and attach them to herself, to repair her own misfortunes, to acquire wealth, and to protect her from being bullied or set upon by persons with whom she may have dealings of some kind or another.

These persons are: the guards of the town, or the police; the officers of the courts of justice; astrologers; powerful men, or men with interest; learned men; teachers of the sixty-four arts; Pithamardas or confidants; Vitas or parasites; Vidushakas or jesters; flower sellers; perfumers; vendors of spirits; washermen; barbers; beggars; and such other persons as may be found necessary for the particular object to be acquired.

The following kinds of men may be taken up with, simply for the purpose of getting their money; men of independent income; young men; men who are free from any ties; men who hold places of authority under the king; men who have secured their means of livelihood without difficulty; men possessed of unfailing sources of income; men who consider themselves handsome; men who are always praising themselves; one who is naturally liberal; one who has influence with the king or his ministers; one who is always fortunate; one who is proud of his wealth; one who disobeys the orders of his elders; one upon whom the members of his caste

Above: Though a woman is reserved, and keeps her feelings concealed, yet when she gets on the top of a man, she then shows all her love and desire. . . a woman during her monthly courses, a woman who has been lately confined, and a fat woman should not be made to act the part of a man.

Facing page: A courtesan should be agreeable to the man who is attached to her, and despise the man who does not care for her. If while she is living with one man, a messenger comes to her from another man, she may refuse to listen to any negotiations on his part. . . she should not leave the man who may be living with her and who may be attached to her.

keep an eye; an only son whose father is wealthy; an ascetic who is internally troubled with desire; a brave man; a physician of the king; previous acquaintances.

On the other hand, those who are possessed of excellent qualities are to be resorted to for the sake of love and fame. Such men are as follows: men of high birth, learned, with a good knowledge of the world, and doing the proper things at the proper times; poets, good story-tellers, eloquent men, energetic men, skilled in various arts, far-seeing into the future, possessed of great minds, full of perseverance, of a firm devotion, free from anger, liberal, affectionate to their parents, and with a liking for all social gatherings, skilled in completing verses begun by others and in various other sports, free from all disease, possessed of a perfect body, strong, and not addicted to drinking, powerful in sexual enjoyment, sociable, showing love towards women and attracting their hearts to himself, but not entirely devoted to them, possessed of independent means of livelihood, free from envy, and last of all, free from suspicion.

Such are the good qualities of a man.

The following are the ordinary qualities of all women: to be possessed of intelligence, good disposition, and good manners; to be straightforward in behaviour, and to be grateful; to consider well the future before doing anything; to possess activity, to be of consistent behaviour, and to have a knowledge of the proper times and places for doing things; to speak always without meanness, loud laughter, malignity, anger, avarice, dullness, or stupidity; to have a knowledge of the *Kama Sutra*, and to be skilled in all the arts connected with it.

The woman also should have the following charecteristics: she should be possessed of beauty, and amiability, with auspicious body marks. She should have a liking for good qualities in other people, as also a liking for wealth. She should take delight in sexual unions resulting from love, and should be of a firm mind, and of the same class as the man with regard to sexual enjoyment. She should always be anxious to acquire and obtain experience and knowledge, be free from avarice, and always have a liking for social gatherings, and for the arts.

The faults of the women are to be known by the absence of any of the above mentioned good qualities.

The following kinds of men are not fit to be resorted to by courtesans: one who is consumptive; one who is sickly; one whose mouth contains worms; one whose wife is dear to him; one who speaks harshly; one who is always suspicious; one who is avaricious; one who does not care for respect or disrespect; one who can be gained over even by his enemies by means of money; and lastly, one who is extremely bashful.

Ancient authors are of the view that the causes of a courtesan resorting to men are love, fear, money, pleasure, returning some act of enmity, curiosity, sorrow, constant intercourse, *Dharma*, celebrity, compassion, the desire of having a friend, shame, the likeness of the man to some beloved person, the search after good fortune, the getting rid of the love of somebody else, being of the same place, constancy, and poverty. But Vatsyayana decides that desire of wealth, freedom from misfortune, and love are the only causes that affect the union of courtesans with men.

Now a courtesan should not sacrifice money to her love, because money is the chief thing to be attended to. But in cases of fear, etc. she should pay regard to strength and other qualities. Moreover, even though she be invited by any man to join him, she should not at once consent to a union, because men are apt to despise things which are easily acquired. On such occasions she should first send the shampooers, the singers, and the jesters who may be in her service, or in their absence the Pithamardas, or confidants, and others, to find out the state of his feelings and the condition of his mind. By means of these persons she should ascertain whether the man is pure or impure, affected or the reverse, capable of attachment or indifferent, liberal or niggardly; and if she finds him to her liking, she should then employ the Vita and others to attach his mind to her. Accordingly, the Pithamarda should bring the man to her house, under the pretence of seeing the fights of quails, cocks, and rams, of hearing the mynah (a kind of starling) talk, or of seeing some other spectacle, or the practice of some art; or he may take the woman to the abode of the man. After this, when the man comes to her house, the woman should give him something capable of producing curiosity, and love in his heart, such as an affectionate present, telling him that it was specially designed for his use. She should also amuse him for a long time by telling him such stories and doing such things as he may take most delight in. When he goes away she should frequently send to him a female attendant, skilled in carrying on a jesting conversation, and also a small present at the same time. She should also sometimes go to him herself under the pretence of some business, and accompanied by the Pithamarda.

Thus end the means of attaching to herself the man desired.

There are also some verses on the subject as follows: 'When a lover comes to her abode, a courtesan should give him a mixture of betel leaves and betel nut, garlands of flowers and perfumed ointments and, showing her skill in arts, should entertain him with a long conversation. She should also give him some loving presents, and make an exchange of her own things with his, and at the same time should show him her skill in sexual enjoyment. When a courtesan is thus united with her lover she should always delight him by affectionate gifts, by conversation, and by the application of tender means of enjoyment.'

II

Of living like a wife

When a courtesan is living as a wife with her lover, she should behave like a chaste woman, and do everything to his satisfaction. Her duty in this respect, in short, is that she should give him pleasure, but should not become attached to him, though behaving as if she were really attached.

Now the following is the manner in which she is to conduct herself, so as to accomplish the above-mentioned purpose. She should have a mother dependent on her, one who should be represented as very harsh, and who looks upon money as her chief object in life. In the event of there being no mother, then an old and confidential nurse should play the same role. The mother or nurse, on their part, should appear to be displeased with the lover, and forcibly take her away from him. The woman herself should always show pretended anger, dejection, fear, and shame on this account, but should not disobey the mother or nurse at any time.

She should make out to the mother or nurse that the man is suffering from bad health, and making this a pretext for going to see him, she should go on that account. She is moreover, to do the following things for the purpose of gaining the man's favour.

Sending her female attendant to bring the flowers used by him on the previous day, in order that she may use them herself as a mark of affection, also asking for the mixture of betel nut and leaves that have remained uneaten by him; expressing wonder at his knowledge of sexual intercourse, and the several means of enjoyment used by him; learning from him the sixty-four kinds of pleasure mentioned by Babhravya; continually practising the ways of enjoyment as taught by him, and according to his liking; keeping his secrets; telling him her own desires and secrets; concealing her anger; never neglecting him on the bed when he turns his face towards her; touching any parts of his body according to his wish; kissing and embracing him when he is asleep; looking at him with apparent anxiety when he is rapt in thought or thinking of some other subject than herself; showing neither complete shamelessness, nor excessive bashfulness when he meets her, or sees her standing on the terrace of her house from the public road; hating his enemies; loving those who are dear to him; showing a liking for that which he likes; being in high or low spirits according to the state that he is in himself; expressing a curiosity to see his wives; not continuing her anger for a long time; suspecting even the marks and wounds made by her nails and teeth on his body to have been made by some other woman; keeping her love for him unexpressed by words, but showing it by deeds, and signs, and hints; remaining silent when he is asleep, intoxicated, or sick; being very attentive when he describes his good actions, and

Above: The signs of the woman's want of enjoyment and of failing to be satisfied are as follows: she shakes her hands, she does not let the man get up, feels dejected, bites the man, kicks him, and continues to go on moving after the man has finished.

Facing page: With increasing assiduity he should dispel her fears, and by degrees get her to go with him to some lonely place, and there he should embrace and kiss her. A woman who meets a man in lonely places, and puts up with the touch of his foot, but pretends, on account of the indecision of her mind, not to be aware of it, should be conquered by patience, and by continued efforts.

reciting them afterwards to his praise and benefit; giving witty replies to him if he be sufficiently attached to her; listening to all his stories, except those that relate to her rivals; expressing feelings of dejection and sorrow if he sighs, yawns, or falls down; pronouncing the words 'Live long' when he sneezes; pretending to be ill, or to have the desire of pregnancy, when she feels dejected; abstaining from praising the good qualities of anybody else, and from censuring those who possess the same faults as her own man; wearing anything that may have been given to her by him; abstaining from putting on her ornaments and from taking food when he is in pain, sick, low spirited, or suffering from misfortune, and condoling and lamenting with him over the same; wishing to accompany him if he happens to leave the country himself or if he be banished from it by the king; expressing a desire not to live after him; telling him that the whole object and desire of her life was to be united with him; offering previously promised sacrifices to the deity when he acquires wealth, or has some desire fulfilled, or when he has recovered from some illness or disease; putting on ornaments every day; not acting too freely with him; reciting his name and the name of his family in her songs; placing his hand on her loins, bosom and forehead, and falling asleep after feeling the pleasure of his touch; sitting on his lap and falling asleep there; wishing to have a child by him; desiring not to live longer than he does; abstaining from revealing his secrets to others; dissuading him from vows and fasts by saying 'Let the sin fall upon me'; keeping vows and fasts along with him when it is impossible to change his mind on the subject; telling him that vows and fasts are difficult to be observed, even by herself, when she has any dispute with him about them; looking on her own wealth and his without any distinction; abstaining from going to public assemblies without him, and accompanying him when he desires her to do so; taking delight in using things previously used by him, and in eating food that he has left uneaten; venerating his family, his disposition, his skill in the arts, his learning, his caste, his complexion, his native country, his friends, his good qualities, his age, and his sweet temper; asking him to sing, and to do other such like things, if able to do them; going to him without paying any regard to fear, to cold, to heat, or to rain; saying with regard to the next world that he should be her lover even there; adapting her tastes, dispositions and actions to his liking; abstaining from sorcery; disputing continually with her mother on the subject of going to him, and, when forcibly taken by her mother to some other place, expressing her desire to die by taking poison, by starving herself to death, by stabbing herself with some weapon, or by hanging herself; and lastly assuring the man of her constancy and love by means of her agents, and receiving money herself, but abstaining from any dispute with her mother with regard to pecuniary matters. When the man sets out on a journey, she should make him swear that he will return quickly, and in his absence should put aside her vows of worshipping the deity, and should wear no ornaments except those that are lucky. If the time fixed for his return has passed, she should endeavour to ascertain the real time of his return from omens, from the reports of the people and from the positions of the planets, the moon and the stars. On occasions of amusement, and of auspicious dreams, she should say 'Let me be soon united to him.' If, moreover, she feels melancholy, or sees any inauspicious omen, she should perform some rite to appease the deity.

When the man does return home she should worship the god Kama and offer oblations to other deities, and having caused a pot filled with water to be brought by her friends, she should perform the worship in honour of the crow who eats the offerings which we make to the names of deceased relations. After the first visit is over she should ask her lover also to perform certain rites, and this he will do if he is sufficiently attached to her.

Now a man is said to be sufficiently attached to a woman when his love is disinterested; when he has the same object in view as his beloved one; when he is quite free from any suspicions on her account; and when he is indifferent to money with regard to her.

Such is the manner of a courtesan living with a man like a wife, and set forth here for the sake of guidance from the rules of Dattaka. What is not laid down here should be practised according to the custom of the people, and the nature of each individual man.

There are also two verses on the subject as follows: 'The extent of the love of women is not known, even to those who are the objects of their affection, on account of its subtlety, and on account of the avarice and natural intelligence of womankind.'

Women are hardly ever known in their true light, though they may love men, or become indifferent towards them; may give them delight or abandon them; or may extract from them all the wealth that they may possess.

III

Of the means of getting money. Of the signs of the change of a lover's feelings, and the ways to get rid of him

Money is got out of a lover in two ways viz. by natural or lawful means, and by artifices. Old authors are of the view that when a courtesan can get as much money as she wants from her lover, she should not make use of artifice. But Vatsyayana lays down that though she may get some money from him by natural means, yet when she makes use of artifice he gives her doubly more, and therefore artifice should be resorted to for the purpose of extorting money from him at all events.

Now the artifices to be used for getting money from her lover are as follows: taking money from him on different occasions, for the purpose of purchasing various articles, such as ornaments, food, drink, flowers, perfumes and clothes, and either not buying them, or getting from him more than their cost; praising his intelligence to his face; pretending to be obliged to make gifts on occasion of festivals connected with vows, trees, gardens, temples, or tanks; pretending that at the time of going to his house, her jewels have been stolen either by the king's guards, or by robbers; alleging that her property has been destroyed by fire, by the falling of her house, or by the carelessness of her servants; pretending to have lost the ornaments of her lover along with her own; causing him to hear through other people of the expenses incurred by her in coming to see him; contracting debts for the sake of her lover; disputing with her mother on account of some expenses incurred by her for her lover, and which were not approved of by her mother; not going to parties and festivities in the houses of her friends for the want of presents to make to them, she having previously informed her lover of the valuable presents given to her by these very friends; not performing certain fes-

tive rites under the pretence that she has no money to perform them with; engaging artists to do something for her lover; entertaining physicians and ministers for the purpose of attaining some object; assisting friends and benefactors both on festive occasions, and in misfortune; performing household rites; having to pay the expenses of the ceremony of marriage of the son of a female friend; having to satisfy curious wishes during her state of pregnancy; pretending to be ill, and charging her cost of treatment; having to remove the troubles of a friend; selling some of her ornaments, so as to give her lover a present; pretending to sell some of her ornaments, furniture, or cooking utensils to a trader, who has been already tutored how to behave in the manner; having to buy cooking utensils of greater value than those of other people, so that they might be more easily distinguished, and not changed for others of an inferior description; remembering the former favours of her lover, and causing them always to be spoken of by her friends and followers; informing her lover of the great gains of other courtesans; describing before them, and in the presence of her lover, her own great gains, and making them out to be greater even than theirs, though such may not have been really the case; openly opposing her mother when she endeavours to persuade her to take up with men with whom she has been formerly acquainted, on account of the great gains to be got from them; lastly, pointing out to her lover the liberality of his rivals. Thus ends the ways and means of getting money.

A woman should always know the state of the mind, of the feelings, and of the disposition of her lover towards her, from the changes of

Above: An ingenious person should multiply the kinds of congress after the fashion of the different kinds of beasts and of birds. For these different kinds of congress, performed according to the usage of each country, and the liking of each individual, generate love, friendship, and respect in the hearts of women.

Facing page: When a man and a woman support themselves on each other's bodies. . . and the woman, sitting on his hands joined together and held underneath her, throws her arms round his neck, and putting her thighs alongside his waist, moves herself by her feet, it is called the 'suspended congress'.

his temper, his manner, and the colour of his face.

The behaviour of a waning lover is as follows: he gives the woman either less than is wanted, or something else than that which is asked for; he keeps her in hopes by promises; he pretends to do one thing, and does something else; he does not fulfil her desires; he forgets his promises, or does something else than that which he has promised; he speaks with his own servants in a mysterious way; he sleeps in some other house under the pretence of having to do something for a friend; lastly, he speaks in private with the attendants of a woman with whom he was formerly acquainted.

Now when a courtesan finds that her lover's disposition towards her is changing, she should get possession of all his best things before he becomes aware of her intentions, and allow a supposed creditor to take them away forcibly from her in satisfaction of some pretended debt. After this, if the lover is rich, and has always behaved well towards her, she should ever treat him with respect; but if he is poor and destitute she should get rid of him as if she had never been acquainted with him in any way before.

The means of getting rid of a lover are as follows: describing the habits and vices of the lover as disagreeable and censurable, with the sneer of the lip, and the stamp of the foot; speaking on a subject with which he is not acquainted; showing no admiration for his learning, and passing a censure upon it; putting down his pride; seeking the company of men who are superior to him in learning and wisdom; showing a disregard for him on all occasions; censuring men possessed of the same faults as her lover; expressing dissatisfaction at the ways and means of enjoyment used by him; not giving him her mouth to kiss; refusing access to her *jaghanai* i.e. the part of the body between the navel and the thighs; showing a dislike for the wounds made by his nails and teeth; not pressing close up against him at the time when he embraces her; keeping her limbs without movement at the time of congress; desiring him to enjoy her when he is fatigued; laughing at his attachment to her; not responding to his embraces; turning away from him when he begins to embrace her; pretending to be sleepy; going out visting, or into company, when she perceives his desire to en-joy her during the day time; misconstructing his words; laughing without any joke, or at the time of any joke made by him; laughing under some pretence; looking with side glances at her own attendants, and clapping her hands when he says anything; interrupting him in the middle of his stories, and beginning to tell other stories; reciting his faults and his vices, and declaring them to be incurable; saying words to her female attendants calculated to cut the heart of her lover to the quick; taking care not to look at him when he comes to her; asking him what cannot be granted; and, after all, finally dismissing him.

There are also two verses on this subject as follows: 'The duty of a courtesan consists in forming connections with suitable men after due and full consideration and attaching the person with whom she is united to herself; in obtaining wealth from the person who is attached to her, and then dismissing him after she has taken away all his possessions'.

A courtesan leading in this manner the life of a wife is not troubled with too many lovers, and yet obtains abundance of wealth.

When a courtesan is resolved to take up again with a former lover, her Pithamarda and other servants should tell him that his former expulsion from the woman's house was caused by the wickedness of her mother; that the woman loved him just as much as ever at that time, but could not help the occurrence on account of her deference to her mother's will; that she hated the union of her present lover, and disliked him excessively. In addition to this, they should create confidence in his mind by speaking to him of her former love for him, and should allude to the mark of that love that she has ever remembered. This mark of her love should be connected with some kind of pleasure that may have been practised by him, such as his way of kissing her, or manner of having connection with her.

Thus end the ways of bringing about a reunion with a former lover.

When a woman has to choose between two lovers, one of whom was formerly united with her, while the other is a stranger, the Acharyas (sages) are of the view that the first one is preferable, because his disposition and character being already known by previous careful observation, he can be easily pleased and satisfied; but Vatsyayana thinks that a former lover, having already spent a great deal of his wealth, is not able or willing to give much money again, and is not therefore to be relied upon so much as a stranger. Particular cases may however arise, differing from this general rule on account of the different natures of men.

There are also verses on the subject as follows: 'Reunion with a former lover may be desirable so as to separate some particular woman from some particular man, or some particular man from some particular woman, or to have a certain effect upon the present lover.'

When a man is excessively attached to a woman, he is afraid of her coming into contact with other men; he does not then regard or notice her faults; and he gives her much wealth through fear of her leaving him.

A courtesan should be agreeable to the man who is attached to her, and despise the man who does not care for her. If while she is living with one man, a messenger comes to her from another man, she may either refuse to listen to any negotiations on his part, or appoint a fixed time for him to visit her, but she should not leave the man who may be living with her and who may be attached to her.

A wise woman should only renew her connection with a former lover if she is satisfied that good fortune, gain, love and friendship are likely to be the result of such a reunion.

Above: The signs of the enjoyment and satisfaction of the woman are as follows: her body relaxes, she closes her eyes, she puts aside all bashfulness, and shows increased willingness to unite the two organs as closely together as possible.

Above: When after the congress has begun the woman raises both of her legs, and places them on her lover's shoulders, it is called the 'yawning position'.

Thus ends this treatise on the art of love

Thus ends the *Kama Sutra* of Vatsyayana, which might otherwise be called a treatise on men and women, their mutual relationship, and connection with each other. It is a work that should be studied by all; both old and young; the former will find in it real truths, gathered by experience, and already tested by themselves, while the latter will derive the great advantage of learning things, which some perhaps may otherwise never learn at all, or which they may only learn when it is too late to profit by the learning.

It can also be fairly commended to the student of social science and of humanity, and above all to the student of those early ideas, which have gradually filtered down through the sands of time, and which seem to prove that the human nature of today is much the same as the human nature of long ago. It has been said of Balzac that he seemed to have inherited a natural and intuitive perception of the feeling of men and women, and has described them with an analysis worthy of a man of science. The author of the present work must also have had a considerable knowledge of humanity. Many of his remarks are so full of simplicity and truth, that they have stood the test of time, and stand out still as clear and true as when they were first written, some eighteen hundred years ago.

As a collection of facts, told in plain and simple language, it must be remembered that in those early days there was apparently no idea of embellishing the work, either with a literary style, a flow of language, or quantity of superfluous padding. The author tells the world what he knows in very concise language, without any attempt to produce an interesting story. From his facts how many novels could be written!

And now, one word about the author of the work, the good old sage Vatsyayana. It is much to be regretted that nothing can be discovered about his life, his belongings, and his surroundings. He states that he wrote the work while leading the life of a religious student (probably at Benares) and while wholly engaged in the contemplation of the Deity. He must have arrived at a certain age at that time, for throughout he gives us the benefit of his experience and of his opinions, and these bear the stamp of age rather than youth; indeed the work could hardly have been written by a young man.

In a beautiful verse of the Vedas of the Christians it has been said of the peaceful dead, that they rest from their labours, and that their works do follow them. Yes indeed, the works of men of genius do follow them, and remain as a lasting treasure. And though there may be disputes and discussions about the immortality of the body or the soul, nobody can deny the immortality of genius which ever remains as a bright and guiding star to the struggling humanities of succeeding ages. This work, then, which has stood the test of centuries, has placed Vatsyayana among the immortals, and on this, and on him no better elegy or eulogy can be written than the following lines:

So long as lips shall kiss, and eyes shall see,
So long lives this, and This gives life to thee.

96